STRANGER
AT HOME

JACOB NEUSNER

STRANGER AT HOME

"The Holocaust," Zionism, and American Judaism

The University of Chicago Press
Chicago and London

JACOB NEUSNER, the author of sixty scholarly
works, fourteen textbooks, thirteen collections
of essays, and the editor of five other books, is
University Professor and Ungerlieder Distinguished
Scholar of Judaic Studies at Brown University.

To Yosef Gorni and the faculty of the Chaim
Rosenberg School of Jewish Studies at Tel Aviv
University and the senior administration of the
Tel Aviv University.

The University of Chicago Press, Chicago 60637
The University of Chicago Press, Ltd., London

Library of Congress Cataloging in Publication Data

Neusner, Jacob, 1932–
  Stranger at home.

  Includes index.
    1. Judaism—United States—Addresses, essays,
lectures. 2. Jews in the United States—Identity—
Addresses, essays, lectures. 3. Holocaust, Jewish
(1939–1945)—Addresses, essays, lectures.
4. Zionism—United States—Addresses, essays,
lectures. 5. Jews in the United States—Attitudes
toward Israel.   I. Title.
BM205.N49   296′.0973   80–19455
ISBN 0–226–57628–0

Contents

Contents

Acknowledgments

Mrs. Lois Atwood, the administrator of the Department of Religious Studies at Brown University, helped me prepare this book in two ways. First, she read the numerous essays which were candidates for inclusion and both helped to eliminate some and also showed me how to order others. Second, she read the book with an eye toward avoiding those usages deemed by us to be "sexist," which, in less enlightened days, were routine in my writing. While it is probable that even after her careful review and mine as well, unwanted formulations may remain, we have done our best to address a single world of men and women, and so to find language appropriate for that chosen frame of discourse.

My graduate student, Mr. Alan Peck, joined in this same labor and also helped in many ways in the planning and execution of this book.

Finally, I wish to acknowledge with deep gratitude the stimulation to review my writings of a thoughtful, not-scholarly, character on American Judaism, Zionism, and "the Holocaust." My colleague, Professor Wendell S. Dietrich, was the one who saw that these several papers—part of a very much larger corpus of writing over twenty-five years, on themes which have been obsessive for me—may be brought together into a single book. Had he not asked me why I had not long ago done so, I should not have imagined that, over twenty-five years, I had worked on what was in fact one problem and spun out a single fabric of reflection on that problem. So I owe the articulated recognition of what I had been doing to this colleague, coworker, and friend, to whom I owe much else as well.

My former students, Professors William Scott Green, University of Rochester, and Richard Samuel Sarason, Hebrew Union College–Jewish Institute of Religion, took the time to read and comment on this book in manuscript. I am grateful for their suggestions.

What helped me to make sense of these papers as a group and to see their logic was a visit to Tel Aviv. There I was able once again to confront the material reality of the Jewish state, to realize that, beyond all the debates, there is the concrete, enduring, and normal life of three million Jews working out their destiny as a nation. That is why I have dedicated this book as I have. For the honor of the invitation to share in that important celebration, for the exceptional and even lavish hospitality accorded to me at that time, and, especially, for the careful hearing accorded to my paper—at such sharp variance with peoples' sense of themselves in Jewish learning in the State of Israel—I express my thanks to my hosts. These include the following: the president and rector of Tel Aviv University, Professors Haim Ben Shachar and S. Abarbanel; the senior administration of the Rosenberg School of Jewish Studies, Professors S. Simonsohn, A. Dothan, and Y. Nini, and their colleagues, in particular Dr. Itamar Gruenwald; my friends Mr. Aharon Amir, Mr. Ari Avnerr; and Dr. Yosef Dan and Dr. E. E. Urbach, present and past heads of the Institute of Jewish Studies of the Hebrew University of Jerusalem, who went to much trouble to accord my speech a full hearing; and, indeed, to all who joined in making the occasion deeply significant for my life and learning. Above all I express thanks to Professor and Mrs. Yosef Gorni, for friendship and hospitality out of all relationship to what is owing among colleagues. Let this book stand as a token of gratitude to people who showed me that you do not have to feel strange at home at all.

I also acknowledge with thanks permission to reprint these papers of mine, granted by the copyright holders, which appeared as follows: "Stranger at Home: An American Jew Confronts the State of Israel," as "A Stranger at Home: An American Jew Visits in Israel," in *Judaism* 11, no. 1 (1962): 27–31. © 1962 by American Jewish Congress; "Freedom's Challenge to Judaism," in *Judaism* 14, no. 1 (1965), 3–11. © 1965 by American Jewish Congress; "Sacred and Secular, Archaic and Modern: The Crisis of Modernity," as "The Way Forward," in *Reconstructionist* 37, no. 6, September 17, 1971, pp. 7–13. © 1971 by *Reconstructionist, Inc.*; "Assimilation and Self-Hatred in Modern Jewish Life," in *Conservative Judaism* 26, no. 1 (1971): 50–60. © 1971 by The Rabbinical Assembly; "The Implications of the Holocaust," in *The Journal of Religion* 53, no. 3 (1973): 293–308. © 1973 by The University of Chicago; "How the Extermination of European Jewry Became 'the Holocaust,'" as "A 'Holocaust' Primer," in *National Review,* August 3, 1979, pp. 975–79. © 1979 by *National Review*; "Jubilee in Tübingen," in *Moment* 3, no. 2 (December 1977): 61–62. © 1977 by *Moment Magazine* Associates; "Are We in Exile?" in *Dimensions in American Judaism* 5, no. 3 (1971): 16–18. © 1971 by the Union of American Hebrew Congregations; "A New Heaven and a New Earth," in *Ideas* 4, no. 1 (1973): 40–48. © 1973 by *Ideas Magazine*; "From Sentimentality to Ideology: The Tasks of Zionism in American Judaism," as the keynote address for the American Jewish Congress Israel Dialogue, July 9, 1979, in Jerusalem. © 1979 by American Jewish Congress; "A Zionism of Jewish Peoplehood," as "Toward a Zionism of Jewish Peoplehood," in *Reconstructionist* 38, no. 8 (1972): 14–21. © 1972 by *Reconstructionist, Inc.*; "The Spiritual Center? The Uses of the Circle-Metaphor," as "The Circle-Metaphor," in *New Outlook* 18, no. 1 (1975): 58–64. © 1974 by *New Outlook*; "Israel and Yavneh: The Perspective of Time," in *New Outlook* 20, no. 1 (1977): 46–52. © 1977 by *New Outlook*; "Judaism and the Zionist Problem," in *Judaism* 19, no. 3 (1970): 311–23. © 1970 by American Jewish Congress; "Zionism and 'The Jewish Problem,'" in *Midstream* 15, no. 9 (1969): 34–53. © 1969 by The Theodor Herzl Foundation, Inc.

Preface

This is a book about American Judaism, not about the destruction of the Jews of Europe ("the Holocaust") or about the creation and maintenance of the Jewish state in the eastern Mediterranean (Zionism). But American Judaism, the world view and way of life of the vast majority of those Americans who regard themselves as Jews, shapes its conceptions of meaning out of the materials of events of Europe and the Near East. These events, far from America's shores and remote from American Jews' everyday experience, constitute the generative myth by which the generality of American Jews make sense of themselves and decide what to do with that part of themselves set aside for "being Jewish." Indeed, stating matters in this way, speaking of a part of the life of an otherwise undifferentiated American, imposes too narrow limits upon our discourse. What is to be called "the myth of Holocaust and redemption" shapes the day-to-day understanding of those who live within the myth and dictates both perceptions and deeds pertinent to the workaday world of ordinary folk. So a sizable sector of the American people sees the world in and along the lines of vision of reality beginning in death, "the Holocaust," and completed by resurrection or rebirth, "Israel."

These essays explore the puzzling frame of mind of people whose everyday vision of ordinary things is reshaped into a heightened, indeed mythic, mode of perception and being by reference to awful events they never witnessed, let alone experienced, and by the existence of a place which they surely do not plan to dwell in or even to visit. Written over a period of nearly twenty years, they turn out to frame and fairly systematically explore the issue I believe to be at the very heart and soul of American Judaism. All together they are meant to do two things and do not claim to do a third. They raise in a vivid way what I believe to be the central questions awaiting confrontation by participants in American Judaism and interpretation by its observers and students. They furthermore undertake to explore the ideological and theological problems presented by the confrontation with these questions, to ask in the manner of an engaged participant those same questions raised at the outset, even to propose initiatives toward the framing of answers to those questions.

But what these papers do not do is gain a stance wholly outside of the phenomenon described and explored. They do not ask questions of analysis and interpretation pertinent to a larger agendum of social theory, let alone of the history of religions. Why do people of the particular and historical profile of American Jews—that is to say, fully acculturated Americans, with a considerable measure of educational accomplishment, yet occupying one of the lower rungs in the ladder of social esteem and forming, if not a pariah people, also no secure sector of the governing and highly regarded echelons of most towns and cities—why do such people urgently construct for themselves a world in which they do not live—an ark they do not plan to stock and float? Why do they draw upon experiences they have not had and do not wish to have for their generative symbols and organizing myths, definitive rites and deeds of a holy way of life? These are questions I do not ask. The reason is that I cannot imagine answering such questions without a frame of social theory and comparison beyond my capacities for construction. So, as I said, I deal with those two matters accessible to someone standing on the inside, near the margins of the group subject to description. I ask critical questions. I offer those answers available to one who asks the questions essentially from the perspective of a person within the frontiers. I make some more or less systematic effort at providing normative ideological analysis of the questions and even point toward a theological response to them. But the issues of comparative analysis and theoretical explanation I do not claim to confront. Those who will do so will, I hope, be much helped by what is done here.

The question to which the myth of "Holocaust and redemption"—the story of the extermination of European Jewry and the creation of the State of Israel—forms a compelling, and, to believers, self-evident, answer is what we have to discern. Indeed, why the slaughter of the Jews of Europe should be turned into "the Holocaust," a term with—again, to participants—self-evident (even "unique") meanings and implications, has to be found out in the context of the life of the people to whom those meanings and implications prove self-evidently unique. What important questions are answered by reference to that component of the normative myth have to be specified. Similarly, why American Jews sustain the contradictory position of deeming the State of Israel to be critical to their own existence as a distinctive, self-sustaining group in American society, and also insisting that they and their future find permanent place within American society, has to be worked out. Here is a strange sort of civil religion indeed. A special question within that larger frame of inquiry, and one to which I devote much attention, is what sort of Zionism can make sense within this contradictory position. For American Jews find themselves Americans in the streets of Jerusalem, but willfully Jews in their own and their neighbors' consciousness and imagination.

Being a minority, and, as I said, not a much admired or emulated minority, these people find themselves persistent strangers, strangers at home, whether the home is here or there, made to feel alien over there, yet more strange at home by what happens always where they are not. Now what is puzzling is not that political events—the destruction of a group, the formation of a national state—should generate dislocation in society and so in peoples' imagination. It is that the state of dislocation should be made into the permanent and, if truth be told, normative condition of a group. Killing off the bulk of Europe's Jews constitutes a social change of profound and lasting consequence. Setting up a Jewish state in the ancient homeland also presents a social change of equivalently fundamental character: social change is symbol-change. The shift in the symbolic life of those Jews fortunate enough to find their way to the Jewish state, the use of the destruction of European Jewry in the self-understanding of that state, the formation of a consequent symbolic structure, with its myth and rites of expression of that myth—these expressions of Israel's civil religion are not difficult to describe and to explain. The incapacity of American Jews to make sense of themselves in the aftermath of these same events, except through the appropriation of exactly the same symbolic structure, myth, and rites— this, as I have said, defines the critical problematic of American Judaism.

To state my case simply: if you want to understand Judaism in America, this is the question you must ask. And if you want to understand what it means to be *like* what it means to be a Jew in America (and I think that meaning encompasses all who see themselves as different from the majority, hence pretty much the whole of America), this is the puzzlement you had best explore. For in the end it is a ubiquitous human dilemma taken up and expressed in a merely idomatic way within American Judaism. But just what that dilemma is and why it takes the forms it does and not some other forms, why, specifically, people choose to work out their sense of themselves and their society in terms essentially irrelevant to their ordinary world and everyday experience—these are the questions others will have to work out.

I can bring you only to the end of that turf on which I too live, the ground which is both not mine and not not-mine, the only land which I know, the only language which I use, but which, language and land both, I am supposed to regard as someone else's. Why I should be a stranger where I think I should be at home, whether in Jerusalem or in Providence, I cannot say. But powerful modes of determining society's norms, both there and here, both without and within, both social and deep within the heart, insist not that I cannot go home again, but that I am not supposed to have a home, not now, not ever, where I am, and, in the nature of things, not anywhere else. That insistence, which takes shape and comes to expression, within American Judaism, in the myth of "Holocaust and redemption," is what makes urgent the question of description and interpretation addressed in these essays of mine. I suspect that the persistent and powerful sense of dissonance, in particular between where I am and the consciousness of who I want to be, is what accounts for the papers' consistency and cogency, despite their composition over a period of nearly twenty years.

Let me now explain the order of the topics and the logic of the book as a whole. These are meant to be transparent.

The discussion is meant to be analytical. But I open with a prologue which is personal. Throughout these papers I attempt to preserve a measured distance between myself and my observations and propositions. So honesty requires that at the outset I state my own reasons for caring about the topic to begin with, and so making observations and offering propositions relevant to it. The thesis of the book is that American Judaism, a way of viewing the world and forming a way of life relevant to the distinctive existential condition of American Jews, is a system removed from participation in the world, a detached and noncathectic way of living in the world. This kind of Judaism does not mediate reality, interpreting and shaping a meaningful mode of human existence. It stands as a barrier between direct and personal participation in Judaic existence. At the very outset, in the prologue, I present my own view of matters, beginning by offering my conclusions. I confront the logically necessary conclusion of the matter: the material reality of the State of Israel contrasted with that condition of alienation which is normal, though which can never be normative, for the Jew of the *Golah*. Perhaps it appears to be ironic that a book on American Judaism has to begin with the encounter with the State of Israel. But the irony is only for a Jew who is no Zionist. For me it is not ironic but quite natural to open the discussion of American Judaism with the confrontation not to be avoided. For the formation of the State of Israel is the greatest political event in the history of the Jewish people since the last coins which read, "Israel's freedom, year one," and "Israel's freedom, year two." Anyone who proposes to reflect upon what it means to be a Jew, upon the ideology of Jewish being and the theology of Judaism, has both to begin and to end with the reality and presence which are not ideology or theology, but prior to both, definitive of the agendum of both. To me these statements are self-evidently true. They present facts. That is why I find myself unable to undertake the work of analysis and comparison which, at the outset, I signaled as the undone task of the book.

In part one I state what I believe to be the ideological and social challenges confronting American Jews and American Judaism. The Jews under discussion are those who do not wholly practice the disciplines of Judaism and also do not wholly neglect them. They take an active part in the life of the Jewish community, its synagogues, organizations, philanthropies, politics, and other practical activities, at the same time living a life essentially void of the spirituality and sensibility of Judaism. They are a community of belief and behavior for they respond in their guts in a single normative way to the world at large. For there in deed and in word is a deeply felt, profoundly compelling consensus among the American Jews of whom I speak, that is, among nearly everyone outside the smallest groups of Orthodox observers, and yet including many of them too. This iron consensus involves, as I said, the twin notions of "Holocaust" and "redemption," bearing meanings everyone knows, leading to conclusions everyone has reached in advance.

Why the myth of "Holocaust and redemption" should take the form which it does, in response, in particular, to the issues of assimilation and self-hatred, and how this particular conception of society and history should serve instead of some other, are questions dealt with in parts two and three. In part two I deal with the matter of whether, in the logic of Judaism, "the Holocaust" makes any difference at all, and I argue that it does not. At the same time I propose an explanation for why the extermination of European Jewry took on for Jews that set of self-evident meanings which, nowadays, it enjoys. What it is that happened so as to turn history into mythic theology, I contend, is to be located in the everyday context of the people for whom events become myth and history becomes theology, and not in the events themselves, which constitute mere history. It is the circumstance of American society and culture which transforms the extermination of European Jewry into "the Holocaust." The reason is simply that it is in this country that "the Holocaust" dominates Jewish public discourse and reliably evokes normative responses and emotions known in advance. That is to say, since in American Judaism "the Holocaust" constitutes one part of the paramount and stable structure of myth and ritual, it is in the context of American Judaism that "the Holocaust" (and its counterpart, the "redemption" formed of Zionism) has to be described and interpreted. The myth is that "the Holocaust" is a unique event, which, despite its "uniqueness," teaches compelling lessons about why Jews must be Jewish and, in consequence of that fact, do certain things known in advance (which have nothing to do with the extermination of European Jewry). The redemptive part of the myth maintains that the State of Israel is the "guarantee" that "the Holocaust" will not happen again, that it is that State and its achievements which give meaning and significance, even fulfillment, to "the Holocaust." The associated ritual is bound up especially in various activities, mostly of a financial character, sometimes of a political one, in support of the State of Israel. The rites of the redemptive myth involve attendance at ritual dinners at which money is given, or, at least, celebrated; endless cycles of work in that same cause; rehearsal of the faith to outsiders and marginal Jews; trips to the State of Israel; and, in sum, the definition of the meaning of "being Jewish" around activities in celebration and support of the existence of the State. So if you want to know why be Jewish, you have to remember that (1) the gentiles wiped out the Jews of Europe, so are not to be trusted, let alone joined; (2) if there had been "Israel," meaning the State of Israel, there would have been no "Holocaust"; and so (3) for the sake of your personal safety, you have to "support Israel." Though you do not have to go live there, it is a mark of piety to feel guilty for not living there (a piety remarkably rare in American Jewry). So this is the myth under discussion, and, briefly noted, these are the accompanying, expressive rituals—both myth and rituals in the service of making sense out of the distinctive group-life of an assimilated and chronically (but not acutely) self-hating group of Jews at best marginal to their historical way of life and world view, that of their ancestors, down to their grandparents. By itself, the destruction of European Jewry forms yet one more, particularly dreadful, moment in a long sequence of tragedy. The theology of Judaism confronted, and confronts, the history of the Jews neither with surprise nor with silence. What was said before, I claim, remains pertinent. Those who claim otherwise are the ones who (quite rightly) point to details of the extermination of European Jewry lacking all precedent in earlier times. These serve as evidence of the "uniqueness" of "the Holocaust." It is from that claim of uniqueness that all else must flow. I do not want it thought that my case is against those who maintain that the destruction of European Jewry is the tragedy that it is. Quite the opposite, those events never leave me, not for an hour, not for a day. That is why their sepulchral presence for me in Tübingen's happy hour has also to be recorded. The issue here is not what actually happened. It is what people today make of what happened. That issue is not to be lost.

The other, and more important, half of the regnant myth of American Judaism, as I said, is the part about "redemption." That Zionist part speaks of the formation and maintenance of the State of Israel as the compensation and consolation for the death of nearly six million European Jews (among more that fifteen million other European civilians). While there are many American Jews to whom Zionism is simply unknown, in fact the redemptive valence imputed to the State of Israel in American Judaism constitutes a judgment of Zionism. American Judaism must be deemed a wholly Zionist Judaism. There then can be no discussion of Zionism within the context of American Judaism without confronting that first and simplest judgment of Zionism upon world Jewry: all those Jews who do not live in the State of Israel are in exile from the State of Israel. My third part's discussion of why American Judaism is as Zionist as it is takes up that formidable, inescapable issue, the issue of *Golah,* or exile, circling, weaving, and bobbing, around that awesome contradiction, drawing near and moving far; but, in the end, all discourse is obsessed and bound up with that simple obvious fact. I discuss, in the context of Zionism in American Judaism, what in part two I treated in the context of "the Holocaust" in American Judaism: what is the place of Zionism in the imaginative life of American Judaism? Here I also (for I am a Zionist too) try to restate what I believe to be the particular meaning and concrete intellectual tasks of Zionism in American Judaism.

The fourth part of the book deals with what sort of Zionist theory is possible for a Judaism and a Jewish community outside of the State of Israel. It is an analysis of this kind of Zionism—a Zionism relevant to a permanent, self-respecting, sustained and ongoing *Golah* community. First I explore the affirmative side to things, the possibility of a Zionism built upon the Jews' sense of forming a people, one people. Such a Zionism makes a place for those Jews who are at home away from Jerusalem. Since the possibilities of a Zionism of this character invariably evoke the complementary conception of an Israeli state as a spiritual center for the Jewish people throughout the world, I turn next to that metaphor. Unhappily, I am able to find little of substance in the notion of a "spiritual center," which consequently gains the quotation marks owed to a fixed idea of imprecision and little substance beyond its service as a symbol. I work this painful matter out as best I can: what sort of Zionist are you outside the State of Israel? What kind of Zionism do you think worth pursuing while engaged in permanent exile? If I thought I had solid answers to these questions, I should offer them. I cannot find suitable replies. Nor is it my place to raise those equally intractable questions confronting my counterparts on the other side of the oceans: what sort of Zionism do you contemplate, outside the nationalism of the State of Israel? And if Zionism is principally, or only, identical with Israeli nationalism, then what do you have to say to the rest of the Jewish world, with its other nationalisms? And what to the rest of your own population, which is not Jewish at all? So, it is clear, I know there is a formidable beam in my eye, which magnifying the mote in the other person's eye will not remove.

The argument is thus fully worked out, as far as I am able, in the first four parts. Its directions and implications are exposed in part five. That is to say, I do conceive that Zionism solved those Jewish problems which it addressed and claimed to be able to solve: assimilation and self-hatred. That is why I am a Zionist. And yet Zionism brought with its success intractable problems of ideology and even of theology. So Zionism constitutes a problem and a dilemma for Judaism. As a Judaist too I have to reckon with these painful matters; I cannot ignore them and I have no solution for them. So there are these two sides to the matter: the Jewish problem, solved by Zionism, and the Zionist problem, addressed to Judaism. Still, the last word is other than ideological. It is personal. But for that reason it is no less relevant to others. For the State of Israel, beyond all theories of Zionism and theologies of Judaism, confronts the contemporary Jew in all of its powerful, glorious reality: its frailty, imperfection, vast failure—thus its material humanity. The burden of this book is that American Judaism lives a life separated from reality by a veil. American Judaism offers a life constructed around symbols which invoke other times and other places, a *Heilsgeschichte* discontinuous with itself.

The concrete and unmediated everyday Jewish life of the Israeli Jew stands in contrast to the Jewish ways of compromise and self-restraint, of small self-deceptions, petty pretense, and little achievements, of the Jews of America. The myth of "Holocaust and redemption" describes the everyday world of Israeli Jews, who day by day confront their own destruction but prepare for it, who concretely, in this world, experience their own achievements and glory in them too. But what reality does that same myth conjure, and what response do those same symbols of death and triumph over death evoke, for people who, in this same context, know a world of exile very like the one destroyed, but who then have formed no other? American Judaism is founded upon the living of life through the lives of other people. It accords the status of a remarkable, puzzling mode of existential being to that same frame of mind which brings to football games people who never exercise at all. With the recognition that, at its foundation, American Judaism is the existential counterpart to a spectator sport, we reach the end of that argument beginning with the simple assertion of the commonality and humanity of that circumstance which, for Jews in this country (and for much of the world), produces Judaism of the American kind.

Beyond this point we cannot go: the recognition that for American Judaism, existence comes mediated and masked. That is how people want things. Perhaps that is how they should be. I do not think that is how they have to be. But who is to say what is good for humanity, in this age in which, perhaps, it is best not to see too well or too much?

I call attention to the glossary of unfamiliar terms, at the end of the book. My hope is that his book will prove interesting both to "insiders" and to "outsiders" (placed in quotation marks, because I know no true insider or outsider to the human issues, idiomatically expressed, of this book). Would that there could be a glossary, also, for the fears, remembered injuries and slights, inescapable nightmares, awful memories, unreal dreams and hopes, of which the myth of "Holocaust and redemption" is made up. But perhaps there need not be a glossary. For alas! who does not understand and talk the language of experience of the human condition? Still, the Jewish language is particular to the Jewish condition. Where others remember and (merely) resent, we weigh the ashes of our dead and from the beginning fear for our (very) future: *O Lord God, what will you give me, for I continue childless, and the heir of my house is Eliezer of Damascus?* Our resentment is of cosmic dimensions. It is always there.

This overview of the book exposes its simple logic: a question and how it has been answered, a human problem and how people have worked out that problem. The question is posed by the situation of Judaism in a free country but in a trying century. The answers were to introduce the conception of "the Holocaust," with its ineluctable lessons, the presence of Zionism, with its inescapable impositions. These are fully stated, as far as I can both describe them and, in more than a little measure, illustrate what it means to participate in them and see the world through the vision evoked by them. At the end, then, there is a reprise and reconsideration of the whole.

So there it is, question, response, reprise. If in reading the book you do not notice which paper was written first, which later on, then you will have entered into the logic of that peculiar situation of humanity described by the lives of Jews in America and explained in so flawed a way by American Judaism.

It remains to note that each unit begins with an introduction, explaining the papers in somewhat more detail and also commenting upon, and criticizing, their principal propositions. So the argument goes on, myself against myself. If you can carry it forward (being Jewish and caring) or can make use of it in the analysis of something of the human condition (being human and caring too), go ahead. Here is how things looked from 1960 to 1980. They did not have to look that way. They do not have to be that way, tomorrow.

J. N.

Providence

December 14, 1979
24 Kislev 5740
The eve of the first candle of Hanukkah, and
my father's twentieth *yahrzeit*.

Prologue

Introduction

If to be a Jew in America is to retreat from confrontation with one's own reality and to seek mediating structures in the experiences of others, if it is explained by myths self-evidently true to the experiences of others, then we must begin with the end. Beyond the theory of "Holocaust and redemption" is the material reality of the Jewish state, which is supposed to perform salvation. Before discourse on theory, we confront that fact in all its concreteness. We move afterward to the realm of therory from the reality of real feelings, concrete perceptions of ordinary things, felt response to workaday existence. So it is right to start this journey out of the stands and on to the field, out of the range of onlookers and into the frame of players in the games of theory, by saying what it means to turn from spectator to player. Here out on the field the player born of a spectator feels out of place. He is not in uniform. In the Land, in the State, supposed to be at home, American Jews find themselves strange and others strangers. This is as it should be. Confronting the message of Land and State which is the statement of Zionism as a redemptive power, American Jews discover they are stranger than they knew before that confrontation. So at the outset let there be some simple truths, painful affirmations, a few obvious points, trivial but materially important facts about what it is to be an American Jew in a Jewish state and afterward. Stranger at home, we go home ever more estranged, having broken the spell, now—paradoxically—seeking vicarious enchantment. That is the story of American Judaism, as far as I can tell it: the tale of people looking for what must find them.

Stranger at Home
An American Jew Confronts the State of Israel

I have traveled the length and breadth of the State of Israel from Eilat to Metullah, from Jerusalem to Safed, from Haifa to the Dead Sea. I have been obsessed with the Land and the State, both as a believing Jew and as an American Zionist.

The more I know about Israel, the less I feel I understand. The more I meet Israelis, the less I comprehend them. The reality of the State and its people overwhelms me, perplexes me, troubles and disturbs me.

The astonishing fact about Israel is that it is what it claims to be, a Jewish state built by Jewish people on Jewish soil and by Jewish labor; a state in which the Hebrew language and the Jewish creative genius form the foundation of national culture; a state in which the Jew is at home, no longer challenged by the gentile to explain who Jews are and why they persist in history, no longer faced with the task of mediating between Jewishness and another culture.

These are facts, no longer hopes, and hence are easy to forget. Perhaps the only time one really faces them is in the first few days in Israel. Afterward, the reality of Israel fades away, because it is commonplace, and one pays more attention to the superficialities of daily life. Each visit to Israel I have faced these facts, and asked myself the question too many Israelis ask, Why do I not settle here? Too much troubled by the question, I seek, and find, the answers in daily life, both at home and in Israel.

At home, this writer is most aware that he is a Jew, because that is how he is distinguished from other Americans, with whom he has so much in common. In Israel, one is mostly an American, or less appropriately, an "Anglo-Saxon" (I think certain exclusive hotels and country clubs would find *that* interesting). Even though I want to feel at home, more often than not I am treated as a foreigner and a tourist: I am an American. In the end, I find myself affirming just that: I am an American, both sentimentally and culturally, and my deepest loyalties are to America.

How then may I, as a Jew, take into account the astonishing facts that the State of Israel realizes? If it is all true, as it is, then how am I to respond?

Anyone might find numerous answers, in the superficialities of daily life there and in the profundities of civilization here. Here I find much that I like, admire, accept, and want to transmit to the future. I do not believe any society has been so open or free, so fundamentally decent, as American society. I do not believe daily life anywhere else can be so easy and relaxed. I do not find any national culture developing with such vigor, variety, or soundness, the proof of which is the eagerness of other nations to appropriate elements of American culture. Hence, furthermore, I find an ideal, a "way of life," unique in human affairs today, and I want to share in the defense of that ideal, which is, quite simply, democracy in political, cultural, social, and religious life. Just as the Israeli easily forgets the astonishing facts represented by Israel, so we regard the unique achievements of American democracy as commonplace, and are more aware of contradicitions of the democratic ideal within American society than of its realizations.

Israelis do not understand the nationalism and patriotism of Jewish Americans, for in no European country was a Jew able to feel that he was part of the "majority" culture; the exceptions, in Western Europe, were few in number, and generally entered the majority by relinquishing ties to their own religious and cultural minority. Israelis generally regard the loyalty of American Jews to America as similar to the loyalty of "Egyptian" Jews to the fleshpots of Pharoah, and similarly reprehensible. It is difficult for the Israelis I met to refrain from warning me of historical facts I know full well, that no other Diaspora community ever was entirely spared, at some points in its history, the rigors of anti-

Semitism. I often replied that security is not available to a people that persists too long in history. No matter where one lives, if he stays there for long enough, times are likely to change, and earlier certainties vanish. I ask only the uninterrupted and generally happy tenure of the Jews in Babylon, longer, in fact, than that of the Jews in Palestine. The Jews in Palestine trace a history, during the First Commonwealth, of about six hundred years, and during the second, of about eight hundred years (measuring from the return under Cyrus to the beginning of the fourth century of the Common Era), while (as far as we can tell) the Jews in Babylon lived under reasonably secure conditions, by comparison to those affecting other peoples in Mesopotamia, from the time of Jeremiah at least until the decline of the Sassanian Empire in the sixth century of the Common Era, eleven hundred years, or even further, until 1948. In truth, security could hardly be the criterion to measure the value of settling among forty million hostile Arabs. Finally, the experience of German Jewry, which felt analogously toward Germany, is hardly decisive, first, because America is not Germany, and has no such black hatred of Jews as part of its nationalism, and second, because if Rommel had won at El Alamein in 1942, Palestinian Jewry would, alas, have had no better fate than Dutch, German, or Italian Jewries. In fact, history proves nothing about the truth of ideas, but renders them, without reference to their rightness, either real or tragic.

Daily life in Israel seemed to me unnecessarily difficult, not only because of the difficulty of making a living, but because of different attitudes toward the conduct of life and standards of right action. It would be discourteous of a visitor to become specific, but on more than one occasion, I felt "Israel for the Israelis."

At times I felt that the xenophobia of Israelis, and, in particular, their disdain for American Jewry, express less a considered judgment than a response to the question, What are *we* doing here? One well-educated young Israeli told me that he would find a certain satisfaction in forced emigration of American Jewry; and, in general, I can see *shelilat hagolah* as little more than a very specific form of xenophobia, expressed also in ridicule of the pronounced American accent in speaking Hebrew, of American ways of dress, even of Americans' insistence on clean kitchens and sanitary facilities. We, for our part, ought not to feel we must criticize the conditions of Israeli life and social intercourse in order to justify our "remaining" in America. I do not think we need to exalt the situation of *Golah,* its cultural and social benefits, in order to defend our status quo. I was born in America, as a part of the third generation of American Jews and an educator of the fourth; I do not feel the necessity to affirm reality, or to promise, even, to write a Babylonian Talmud in order to justify life in our modern Babylon. "Blessed is he who inspires the inhabitants of a place with love for it." I neither affirm nor deny destiny, but, only, accept it.

I think that a far more significant problem than American *aliyah* or Israeli *yeridah* (since 1948, more Israelis have settled in the Western hemisphere than have Americans, both north and south of the border, immigrated to Israel) is the problem of future relationships between the State and the Diaspora, particularly the American Diaspora. The tragic necessities of the past decades, of saving a remnant and helping them to build a homeland, have demanded an awful price in blood. They have, however, only begun to manifest the price to be paid by the living. The American Jewish community has generously responded to Israel's legitimate financial requirements, and will, I hope, continue to do so for decades. It has received in exchange a great and welcome return: the State itself, its extraordinary achievements, its successful refutation of any and every anti-Semitic canard against the Jewish people. In truth, whatever factual basis anti-Semitism ever had in economic, social, political, or cultural life has been swept away. Jews can no longer be accused of economic parasitism, for they have drained swamps and planted deserts; of social or cultural parasitism, for they have recovered and enhanced their own heritage; of political impotence, for they have reentered the drama of history. All this has been achieved by the State of Israel. The State has, moreover, ended the corroding fear of Jewish homelessness, and however secure the Jews are in America, they have shared that fear if they have read history or the daily newspaper. Israel owes absolutely nothing to American Jewry, and can never be properly repaid for the blood and iron it has lavished to create and sustain itself. I think a great part of American Jewish consensus has to do with the pride and affirmation of American Jewry toward the State and the Zionist cause. In this sense, Israel has served to unify American Jewry, to give its disparate elements a common cause and a common purpose. Finally, the cultural benefits of the State have only begun to reach and fructify our community life.

Israelis, on the other hand, have too little awareness of how much they have given American Jews, and have a sense of obligation that is neither appropriate not affirmative. They see themselves as takers, not givers, and such a self-image does not lead to pride or love. I think another part of Israeli xenophobia may be therefore explained by the Israeli's need to show his independence of his "rich American" guests. "We may be dependent on your money," I was told, "but we will not therefore kowtow to you." (Alas, not a few tourists expect just that.) Nonetheless, the interest most Israelis seem to have in the *Golah* communities is apparently limited by Israeli needs for money and manpower. "Be kind to tourists, they bring hard currency," a poster for children reads; and another, "Every tourist is a potential immigrant." I found very little curiosity about the development of American Jewish life, except as related to Israeli affairs; very little interest in non-Zionist activities in general; and none whatever in our hopes for American Jewry's future.

Furthermore, I regretted to find that Israelis are far less prepared to support voluntary communal activities than American Jews are. When a perfectly legitimate social welfare institution or cultural activity requires support, the first and primary source of financial support is either the government—or the *Golah*. It is certainly true that Israelis have much, much less to give. Giving, however, is measured not only by the size of the gift, but by the benefit to the giver. For example, a certain synagogue in Jerusalem was built mainly by American Jews. When two women who had shared in the project asked the president of the congregation why no landscaping had been done for the building (now standing for more than a decade on one of Jerusalem's main streets), he replied that they ought to ask their husbands to raise the funds. (Indeed, the synagogues pay their rabbis abysmal salaries, most of which come from government funds.)

Seeing themselves, however, inaccurately, as takers and not givers, Israelis apparently see the need to defend whatever they do against moderate and intelligent criticism. They appeal all too often to clichés in order to explain deficiencies. An old story, out of the 1930s, tells about an American who is shown through the new subway system in Moscow. He is impressed by the marbled halls, the immaculate floors, and displays of fine art on the walls, and asks, "This is all very lovely, but where are the subway trains themselves?" "And what about the Negroes in the South?" his guide exclaimed. In Israel, I found two stock replies to the most gentle criticism: an appeal first, to "two thousand years of *Golah*," or alternatively, to "the first Jewish state after two thousand years"; or, second, to the relative youth of the country, and its obviously formidable achievements in so few years. Israel is, however, not a great deal younger than the organized American Jewish community, which for all practical purposes may be dated at about 1880 (Reform and Conservative institutions) or 1900 (Orthodox institutions). In any case, how long does it take to clean the garbage that litters the streets in so many cities? I once asked why the newest and most modern apartment houses invariably have obvious and malodorous garbage cans in the front entry, instead of at the back door, and was accused of being a Jewish anti-Semite or an assimilationist. Indeed, one of the costliest charges of building the State has been paid by the Jews' ancient, resourceful capacity to laugh at themselves.

As I said, the problem that troubles me most is the relationship between the State and the American *Golah*. It is fashionable in Israel to ridicule the Jewish Agency, but what I know of its work impresses me. It is actively interested in bringing *Golah* Jews to Israel, and I think its interest is not only *aliyah* or potential leadership in pro-Israeli activity, but also in a cultural and national renaissance, based on the foundation of Israeli realities and Hebrew culture, throughout the Jewish world. I heard a speech by an Agency official, on the importance of Jewish education everywhere, in which the attraction of Castro for South American Jewish youth was described as a great calamity. That official, and his colleagues, voiced concern for the future of South American Jewry not on account of specific Israeli interests, but on account of the interest of the Jewish nation everywhere. The Agency's work has only just begun. If, as I believe, a Jew who has visited Israel for any substantial period is fundamentally changed in his or her attitude toward himself or herself as a Jew and toward the potentialities of Jewishness and Judaism, then the importance of the Jewish Agency's program is greatly enhanced. A Jew who has seen the State, the Land, and the people must be utterly different from a Jew who has not. The Agency, for all its imperfections, is one effective means of bringing Israel and its benefits into the lives of Jews everywhere.

I do not understand the State of Israel yet, but I understand that the fact of its existence is a caesura in Judaic existence. So I find myself compelled to rethink the meaning of the Jewish faith and of Jewish destiny because of that fact. That is why I shall return, I hope, to Israel many times, not because of what I could ever hope to give to the Jewish state, but because of what the Jewish state has already given me.

Part One

The Problematic of Judaism in America

Identity, Self-Hatred, and the Crisis of Community

Introduction

The power of American Judaism, proved by its veritable self-evidence to the generality of American Jews, flows from its capacity to answer urgent questions present in the depths of the social and imaginative being of American Jews. The pathos of American Judaism is the ambiguous character of the answers. The appropriateness of American Judaism is that the ambiguity accurately replicates the human condition of the people to whom that Judaism addresses itself: ambiguous and ambivalent. For the setting and condition to begin with are defined by the character of America and of the Jews' place in America. America is a free country. The Jews are a minority in a country which affords choice to be what one wants unrestricted by political restraint and social norm. Yet, it must immediately be added, once one does make a choice—and people have choices made for them, which they confirm from day to day—there are significant restrictions. While not wholly political, they invariably are of a powerful, social character.

Whether or not the Jew who ceases to be Jewish puts down one burden only to take up some other I cannot say. But the Jew who is socially and psychologically Jewish assuredly bears a considerable burden. There is, first, the encompassing fact of constituting a minority, difficult for adults, acutely painful for growing children. There is, second, the fact that the particular minority to

which Jews adhere is not one which enjoys high status or un-
challenged self esteem. Anti-Semitism is only the acute expression of what is a chronic and quite normal condition of disesteem.
So, bound up with the identity of being Jewish, the personal mode
of identification as a Jew (with predictable and inescapable
meanings adhering thereto) is the condition of dissonance. This is
between personal esteem and social degradation (not too strong a
word at all); between what the individual may achieve and what
belonging to the group costs. The individual is not a pariah. The
group is a pariah people. That enduring condition of the Jewish
people in America changes in one important way. The individual
no longer finds it necessary to accept the status of the group. Yet,
it is clear, there are vast numbers of individuals and families who
do identify themselves together as, and with, the Jewish group.
So an element of free choice has to be taken into account.

Freedom poses a vigorous challenge to Judaism. That is the
argument of the first paper here, "Freedom's Challenge to
Judaism," which sets the stage for the whole book which follows.
"Assimilation and Self-Hatred in Modern Jewish Life" spells out
what freedom means for American Jews. This paper counts up
the psychological costs of acculturation into a society which accords the individual everything, but the group only some few,
measured things. The costs of acculturation, for reasons carefully
spelled out, prove a heavy burden on the self-esteem of the
American Jew. They provoke a considerable response in that
mode of self-disesteem known as self-hatred. For American Jews
self-hatred is a chronic ailment; America in the 1950s, '60s, and
'70s vastly differs from Europe in the 1920s and '30s, in which the
conception of self-hatred was invented to describe a Jewish
pathology, an acute one at that.

What freedom means for American Judaism is worked out in
"Sacred and Secular, Archaic and Modern: The Crisis of Modernity." There I draw the contrast between the ways in which
Judaism aforetimes filled with meaning the various categories of
the holy life—the holy way of life, the holy man, the holy people,
the holy doctrine (here, Torah)—and the meanings with which the
same categories are infused by American Judaism in the myth of
"Holocaust and redemption." For from some perspectives there
are continuities. But from others we see stunning discontinuities.

No discussion of the place of Zionism and "the Holocaust" in

American Judaism can make sense without close attention to what has happened, in its own frame of reference, to Judaism itself. That is why, in this paper, I carefully but briefly define the meanings of the principal descriptive categories of the religion Judaism, and then spell out those facts which contemporary American Jewish life supplies for those same descriptive categories. The holy way of life was lived personally, individually, not vicariously; without the mediation of experts but only through their guidance. The holy man was a scholar and a saint. The holy people knew precisely who they were: the center of history, the heart of humanity. The holy faith was self-evidently true. In American Judaism nothing now is the same. Certainty is gone, so too all traits of classicism. With the recognition of that fact, the asking of the question confronting American Judaism is complete and exhausted. Then must come the two answers which form one salvific assertion, "the Holocaust," redemption. To describe these answers and to explain how they resolve the question posed by context and existence to American Judaism and asked by Jews of American Judaism becomes the task of the rest of the book.

2

Freedom's Challenge to Judaism

The central issue facing Judaism in our day is whether a long-beleaguered faith can endure the conclusion of its perilous siege. Our faith, during the past century the object of assault from other religions, from academic scholarship, under social and political pressure of all kinds, suddenly confronts a day when it has in many places entered the inchoate cultural establishment. Thus a wholly new attitude toward Judaism characterizes many Christian groups. The determinedly uninformed slanders against it by scholars of religion in antiquity, and of the several disciplines of the social sciences, have long since been discredited, and even so distinguished an anti-Judaist as Arnold J. Toynbee finds it necessary to revise, retract, and reconsider allegations which even fifty years ago were commonplace in the academic world. In this country, moreover, external pressures upon Jews to confront the fact of being Jewish diminish from day to day.

If all this seems entirely obvious, it is equally clear that neither the Jew nor Judaism has yet reflected upon the implications of the current situation. The major issues within Judaism seem mostly to emerge from the debates of half a century ago, and the major concerns of the Jews retain the obsolete qualities of the siege-mentality. Both focus upon the question of survival, and within the debates on Judaism the court of final appeal is frequently not truth or reality but the usefulness of a given notion for preservation of the faith. Thus what people *can* accept is argued with greater vehemence than whether what they *do* accept is true. And for the average Jew, the chief Jewish issue is phrased in wholly ethnic terms: whether children marry Jews is more important than whether they build Jewish homes, whether people live in Jewish neighborhoods matters more than whether the neighborhoods in which they do live are places of dignity and commonplace justice. Thus the sociological issues of Jewish life as well as theological ones deal less with the content of Jewish teaching and Jewish living than its form, more with the "survival" than the spiritual prosperity of the Jew and Judaism.

I wonder whether Jewish history can provide an example of a Jewish community more ethnocentric, and less religiously concerned, than our own. It is true that Jews have always retained a very vivid sense of their separateness from other groups in society. Yet it is difficult to locate a Jewish community in the past which placed such special stress on separateness alone, and which seemed so little interested in the spiritual potentialities or moral implications of that separateness, as our own. Never before has the purpose, for example, of taking a Jewish mate been so ignored, or the fact of doing so been made so crucial. Never has the adjective "Jewish" been so lavishly bestowed on institutions and "causes" so remote from the meaning of that adjective. Indeed, in the free and open society of America, the Jew seems far more conscious of the fact that he is a Jew, and only this, than he could possibly have been in ancient *Eretz Yisrael,* where human issues were debated in a particularly Jewish idiom, or in Babylonia, where the foundations of a peculiarly Jewish society were laid down by men who spoke almost always of "a man" and very rarely of "a Jew."

One may well suspect, therefore, that the reason American Jews who are actively engaged in Jewish community affairs lay such heavy emphasis on Jewish ethnicism is that they have left little other than a visceral ethnic consciousness (and a diminishing one at that). The more profound one's appropriation of Judaism and the more deeply one's life is influenced by Jewish belief and practice, the less important the ethnic connection *per se* appears to be and the more openly one finds oneself a man among men, a *Yisroel-mensch* ("Jewish-person"), in Hirsch's felicitous phrase, among many kinds of human beings. The true result of commitment to Judaism is commitment to God and the Torah. Devotion to God unites the heart of one person with that of another, whatever the beginnings and place in life; study of the Torah yields truths appropriate to a great many people and opens the heart of the Jew to humanity, for it forces attention upon the central realities of the human condition. When, for example, one examines the language of the rabbis of the Talmud, one finds it addressed quite commonly to "a man," quite rarely, except where the context of law or theology demands it, to "a Jew." Thus, R. Yohanan ben Zakkai asked his students: "What is the way in which *a man* should walk?"—not *a Jew;* and the answers likewise concerned human qualities (*middot*) on which no specifically Jewish claim was laid. The Torah, which is our most special possession, is at the same time the means by which we come to be most human. The commandments, which set our conduct of life apart from that of others, were intended, we are taught, "to purify the heart of man," not "to preserve the Jewish people" or to insure the persistence of a special "way of life." But for our place and time what was central has become peripheral, and what was once the obvious and almost irrelevant by-product has become the heart of the matter.

The paradox of our situation is, therefore, the poverty of our spiritual life, the easy access to freedom we no longer choose to exercise, the ironic emphasis on "Jewishness" when the world will listen attentively when addressed by Judaism. We who preach brotherhood so self-righteously to our fellow-citizens preserve in our hearts the least edifying part of our heritage, the hostility to gentiles which in less fortunate ages could at least be understood, if not condoned, against the background of obsessive hatreds. One hears Jews speak quite freely of all non-Jews as *"goyim,"* which is not always a complimentary epithet, while those complex differences which separate one gentile from another, which make of one a Christian and of another a pagan, or a fascist or a secularist, are ignored. One sees the preservation of Jewish neighborhoods and social facilities as unwalled ghettos in towns where Jews are freely accepted into the social life of the general community, and one will look in vain in those ghettos for marks of authentic Jewish living. One finds frail efforts to define "Jewishness" in trivial terms, efforts which are oblivious to the fact that what we think of as uniquely "Jewish" is frequently the result of a particular social experience. We have thus translated sociological realities into teleological desiderata, and begin to believe that the chosen people is separate from other peoples because it does not (or did not) indulge in drunkenness and educates children to be bright. Whatever the relationship of Judaism to Jewish society and culture has been, it was never the source of hostility to mankind (even for sound, monotheist reasons), nor was it the means by which the Jew was abstracted from humanity. Judaism did not create the idea of a ghetto; a hostile Christian society did. Judaism did not exalt the separateness of Jewry, but called upon the Jew to bear witness to God in the midst of life, to sanctify His name among humanity. If one of the natural by-products of Jewish law has been the tendency of Jews to live near one another, the reason was the need to be able to walk to worship, or to live in close proximity to religious fellowship, not only in order to ensure that one Jewish child meet another for the ultimate purpose of matrimony.

The real test of Judaism has yet, therefore, to be faced: it is whether Judaism can flourish when unnatural conditions of persecution or oppression do not prevail, but when freedom does. Is Judaism a frail flower that can live only when protected in a hothouse, or is it hardy enough to grace perennially the garden of humanity? Obviously, both the Jew and Judaism have stood firm against external threat. In times of stress even neurotic people find a purpose for life, and the battlefield is a happy place for psychotics. But under normal conditions only the strong and healthy can endure, for that is what is "normal" about normality. As far as the Jews are concerned, our future as a distinct group will depend not upon what we make of our history or ethnic diversity, not upon unnatural institutional devices intended to ensure a social isolation most Jews do not want or even regard as an advantage, but upon what happens to our religious tradition.

We cannot, moreover, allow ourselves the cheap luxury of longing for a return to an earlier, simpler age. Freedom is far better than any other condition, better for humanity and for society, and therefore it must be the better way for faith as well. And a free and open society cannot be built among hostile and suspicious tribes, forced by accident of history to share a common hunting ground. It depends not on a new form of "tribalization" but its very opposite: a renewed appreciation for what breaks down the walls that separate different kinds of men and makes them one, one in the common challenges of life, one in the confrontation of death, one in the pursuit of a worthy way of spending one's years on earth.

The real issue confronting American Judaism is going to be what Judaism has to offer the Jews so to enhance and ennoble, to sanctify, their lives, that, faced with many options, they will remain loyal to the faith of their parents, not out of disdain for that of others, but out of love for their own. So far, as I have emphasized, American Judaism has persisted although the Jews have largely ignored it, and where they have attended to it they did so out of a determination not to be something other than Jewish, come what may. But American society is opening, not closing, and we are going to see a day in which we live in a shared society and in which Judaism will be welcomed to make its contribution to that society, both through the human exemplars it molds and through the abstract truths it professes. In that day, Jews will ask what is good for the open society, and will believe, as I do not think they do now, that what is good for the open society is good also for them.

I have no doubt whatever that Judaism will flourish in that coming society if Jews appropriate and embody it truly and thoughtfully, because in the past our greatest achievements have resulted from situations of openness in which the consciousness of the Jew was directed not toward "Jewishness" but toward *humanity*. I have a deep conviction, moreover, that we shall err if we despair of our continued prosperity in freedom. We cannot abdicate the present hope for a free society in favor of the gloomy eschaton promised by totalitarianism (Communism, for example), or tribalism, even in the form of parochial ethnocentric religion.

The reason for my certainty of Judaism's viability in freedom is that I discern at present the historical conditions which in the past produced our most lasting monuments, the Bible and the Talmud. The one came out of *Eretz Yisrael*, the other out of Babylonia. The former was the creation of men whose cultural situation was, like that of the contemporary State of Israel, both natural and normal. The prophets, for example, were able to condemn because they had hopes for improvement and did not fear for the "survival" of the people they castigated. The raw material for culture was provided by commonplace life in a small corner of humanity, and in the hands of the prophets current events in

Jerusalem or Tekoa, because of their very embeddedness in one place, could be transformed into archetypal dramas of universal implications. Ancient Israel could be paradigmatic for the ages precisely because of its normality, its commonplace quality, which rendered Jerusalem into "anywhere" and Tekoa into "every place." In the State of Israel today, too, Jews are free to look upon themselves once again not as Jews but as human beings. They are therefore able, as no Diaspora Jew can be, to confront the teachings of Judaism and to receive them not by virtue of historical or ethnic imperatives but because they make sense; to reject them, if they will, because they do not make sense, without the fear that the ephemeral criteria of a living generation may destroy the heritage of centuries for coming ages. The Diaspora Jew can never achieve freedom from this particular fear, because, unlike the Israeli, he or she can never be sure that descendants even a generation later will have access to what has been rejected. In Israel, too, the artifacts of Judaism form the foundation of culture and may be seen as they truly are, as external formulations of intangible realities. In Israel alone can this be so, can the Sabbath be observed as a day of rest rather than as a day for the preservation of the people (as Ahad Ha'Am saw it) or for some other purpose. In Israel alone Judaism ceases to be a "religion," a body of dogmas and beliefs, and becomes what it always was, a "tradition" about about how life should be lived and society should be conducted. And therefore I hope that Israelis can teach us what it means to be a *Yisroel-mensch*, what kind of distinctive society must emerge from the teachings of our faith, what sort of unique people are the harvest of Judaism when Judaism may act unmodulated on the formulation of society and culture.

The Talmud, on the other hand, was the creation of a Jewish community which, in its way and age, was no less free than that in ancient Israel or the contemporary Diaspora. Babylonian Jewry lived as a distinctive group in a country of minorities and without majority. Babylonia sheltered Greeks, Macedonians, and various kinds of Semites, including Arabs, descendants of the cuneiform culture of ancient Babylonia, Iranians, and Jews. These minorities lived sometimes in villages dominated by one group but sometimes also in cities shared by many groups. Indeed, the Talmudic discussions of the Sabbath limits *(eruvin)* presuppose that Jews and pagans were living in the same alleyways and courtyards. Not only were ethnic groups varied but religions were even more so. Within the Babylonian parallelogram the following religions were practiced *ca.* 250 C.E.: Mazdaism (Zoroastrianism), Christianity, Buddhism, Judaism, Mandeanism, and Manichaeism, while numerous cults of both the Hellenistic and the Iranian idioms flourished in the service of specific deities. Moreover, except for the few years in which the Sassanian monarchy established itself, and for some isolated disturbances in the fourth century, Babylonian Jewry lived mainly unmolested and usually quite prosperously from the time of Ezekiel to that of Mohammed (I do not speak here of what happened afterward). Jews fought in Seleucid armies, which presupposes loyalty to that government; they supported the Parthian cause vigorously; and under the Sassanians they apparently found little to complain about. The only major qualification to this rule is that the Jews had to behave in a manner congruent with Mazdean sensitivities, particularly with reference to treatment of corpses and use of fire, but these do not seem to have been substantial hardships except when the government, or state-church, chose to make them so.

Thus, like the Jews in *Eretz Yisrael,* Babylonian Jewry enjoyed many centuries of peace and prosperity, and religious and cultural institutions of Babylonian Jewry traced a continuous history of over a thousand years. To be sure, Babylonian society in the Talmudic period was not an open one in the sense that one was received as an unencumbered individual everywhere one might go. But it was, nonetheless, a society of minorities, where many groups lived active group-lives in a manner not greatly different from that of the several ethnic communities in New York City, for example.

What distinctively characterized Babylonian Jewry was its sense of ethnic identity, however, which was, I believe, more similar to that of American Jewry than to that of Israelis. The reason is obvious: Babylonian Jewry lived in constant contact with non-Jews, and had to modulate its affairs to take account of the ideas and attitudes of non-Jews. Babylonian Jewish leaders were, therefore, men who had mastered not only the traditional Jewish disciplines but also the ancient cultural traditions of Babylonia itself. Samuel, for example (and he is the best example), was a master of the two sciences most highly developed in

Babylonia from ancient times, medicine and astronomy. He lived in an age of considerable cultural interchange. The regnant Shah-an-Shah, Shapur I (241–272), was a powerful, successful monarch, who advanced the frontiers of Sassanian Iran almost to the ancient limits of the Achemenids and maintained a peaceful and prosperous empire. What is especially striking is that he was greatly interested in cultural and scientific matters, and Iranian tradition credits him with including in the corpus of Zoroastrian literature tractates on all manner of scientific and cultural subjects, including lore from India and Greece. He was a man of broad culture, therefore, who took a keen interest in the affairs of his subject peoples (as Jewish tradition testifies in the numerous stories of Samuel and Shapur) and sought out the wisdom that might be derived from each of them for the common advantage of the empire. Furthermore, Babylonia was the center of religious ferment, particularly expressed in the development of a renewed Zoroastrian faith by the priest Kartir, and, of great interest, the creation by Mani of a syncretistic religion based on Iranian, Christian, and Hellenistic beliefs (and, in the east, on Buddhist ones as well). Manichaeism, like Islam later on, used the resources of many religions to construct a single faith which all might happily adopt. This was Mani's intention. This was what Shapur, too, hoped for when he encouraged Mani's preaching, for a syncretistic religion might serve to unify his diverse empire.

The importance of all this for contemporary Judaism cannot be missed. The great creative age in Talmudic Judaism was the third century, when Rav and Samuel in Babylonia (and Yohanan in Palestine) transformed a book of laws, the Mishnah of Judah the Patriarch, into the constitution for the whole society of diverse people. Although Babylonia did possess centers of rabbinic Judaism before *ca.* 220, when Rav returned it is quite clear that Babylonian Jews were not all subject to rabbinic law; we need only look at the walls of the Dura synagogue, the numerous stories of disobedience to both Tannaitic and Amoraic injunctions, and the conduct of the Babylonian Exilarch, to be certain of that fact. But by the end of the third century it seems most likely that most Babylonian Jews did accept the authority of the rabbinic interpretation of Scripture, including law. This took place not during a time of persecution or during an age in which Jews turned their backs on the culture of other peoples, but in an age in which people freely exchanged ideas and in a country in which the broadest range of cultures and faiths was encouraged to flourish. The Talmud was not, therefore, the product of a wholly closed society but of a society that was in many ways open to the world. The very emphasis on the importance of law in that society, which is so striking to modern students of Talmud, may best be understood from this perspective. The rabbis of the Talmud were trying to find the most neutral terms in which to define Jewish society, and these terms were discovered not in the ephemera of belief but in the lasting patterns of everyday life, patterns which might be transferred from place to place and culture to culture because they encompassed the trivial realities in which men spend most of their time. Paradoxically, the rabbis of the Talmud spoke, as did the prophets of ancient Israel, to the commonplace situation of humanity, and in so doing they addressed themselves to the ages. This is important to remember, therefore: the people to whom the rabbis of the Talmud addressed themselves were, like American Jews today, living in a society which offered many options, and in a world which questioned not malevolently but interestedly what Jews thought and why.

I do not for one instant suggest that present-day American Jewry is to be equated with Babylonian Jewry, nor is today's Israel quite the same as that of ancient times. Israel the State has yet to produce its first Isaiah, just as American Jewry has yet to find its Samuel. But what is important is that both ancient Israel and ancient Babylonia give very impressive evidence that Judaism will thrive in freedom, freedom from excessive ethnic self-consciousness, as in the State of Israel today, freedom to learn from and compare oneself with many different cultural possibilities, as in the United States today. I do not fear, therefore, the opening of American society, but welcome it. I look forward to the very rich and interesting contribution that *Yisroel-menschen* may make to such a society. I do not despair that we can do nothing except within ghetto walls, nor do I believe that the best conditions for our survival are unhealthy ones. Judaism's history proclaims the opposite: the Jews are human beings, and therefore flourish best in freedom. Judaism is a religion for humanity, and therefore offers its most enduring truths to an age in which humanity prospers, which must be an age of openness in society, of breadth of cultural alternatives, and of depth of intimacy between group and group.

I realize that the optimism and belief in progress which this viewpoint presupposes have ceased to be stylish in many circles. It is more commonplace to hold, for example, that the most crucial aspect of Judaism is its ability to help people to confront their existential agonies, rather than, as I have urged, its capacity to make Jewish people more human and humane. It is modish these days to lament the conditions of humanity rather than to discover in the human situation in what seems a darkening age the evidences of growing freedom and a renewed union of humanity. I need not defend myself, however, for holding outdated opinions, and for urging the reconsideration of ancient cultural and social options. My conviction that freedom is an absolute good seems to contradict the trends, much lamented by this writer among others, toward the assimilation of Jews into the undifferentiated masses. The obvious response to threatened assimilation seems to many to require the erection of walls for defense of the group and the emphasis on those aspects of our tradition which separate Jews from others for no very substantial reason. Yet I do not believe that our destiny will be determined in the end by the laws of sociology, but by the will of God. We American Jews, brands plucked from the burning, were not preserved from the Holocaust so that we might become apostates and turn to the worship of the no-gods of ethnic chauvinism or materialism. A tradition which sustained so many generations of Jews under the most dreadful circumstances retains within itself enduring power and rich promise, despite the unhappy auguries of a given moment. If American Jewish masses do not today demonstrate that fact, one need not lose confidence in the eternity of the Torah. For the testimony of the ages yields in the end a verdict of hope and not despair.

3

Sacred and Secular, Archaic and Modern

The Crisis of Modernity

The way of Torah led the Jewish people to the threshold of modernity and to the shores of America—to, but not beyond. The classic mythic structure of Judaism did not endure in its old form. In times past all Jews saw the world through the mythic prism of the rabbinic Torah. That is, they viewed the world as created by God. They saw themselves as Israel, to whom Torah had been revealed. The looked forward to the coming of the Messiah. These were "facts" they knew to be true, not beliefs they held "on faith." Of greatest importance, whatever happened in everyday life could be explained according to the comprehensive Torah-myth.

If we examine important elements of the Torah-myth and see how they have developed in American Judaism, we notice the signs of thoroughgoing change.

First: the holy way of life. In classical Judaism the holy way was lived by everyone. Each man studied for himself, prayed for himself, fully and personally participated in the life of Torah. (Women are essentially excluded from the vital center of the Judaic system, so when I refer to "man," I mean males, not females.) Today to be a Jew means to join a Jewish organization. But the things one does after joining that organization (except the synagogue)—bowling, or theater parties, or luncheons for the women—have little to do with the things the organization accomplishes.

Second: the holy man, the rabbi. In classical Judaism the rabbi was a scholar and a saint. He was learned, and he was also a holy man. In American Judaism, few rabbis achieve a significant level of scholarship, even in the classical Judaic texts, and no rabbi is looked upon as a holy man or as a miracle-worker.

Third: the holy people, Israel. In classical Judaism, Israel was a singular people on the earth, unique and holy, beyond the power of the nations to judge or criticize. The classical, or archaic, Jew had no difficulty defining who was Israel, or what it means to be a Jew, or why one should be a Jew. It was a privilege, a joy, an honor. In modern times the Jewish people entered a lingering crisis of identity, as the single religious interpretation of being Jewish ceased to persuade most Jews, and many explanations were offered in its place. Why should I be Jewish? What does it mean to be a Jew? These now are important questions.

And add to them one more factor: today Jews are seriously concerned with the opinions of gentiles about Jews. Since being Jewish in a measure sets a person apart from the majority, makes him different, and since that difference is no longer seen to be destiny, but merely otherness, Jews have placed a negative value upon being Jewish. They have, in other words, come to hate themselves as Jews, or to hate that part of themselves that makes them Jewish. Jewish self-hatred and the crisis of identity of modern Jews go hand in hand. So the holy people has become indeed profane, worldly, conscious of its unholiness, of its *not* being separate from the peoples.

Fourth: holy faith. In classical Judaism, theological ideas were, by and large, not systemized, but were contained and expressed in aphorisms, folk sayings, wise moral teachings. That was because the systematization of faith was unnecessary. Since faith was so whole, complete, thoroughly integrated, it could not be abstracted from the very fabric of everyday life, set apart, and "thought about." Theology was not written, because it was lived. Myths were not stories to be told, because they were part of the very meaning of life. American Judaism has brought forward a number of sophisticated theologians, who systematize, defend, formulate, organize "faith" in philosophical terms. They no longer express or convey the faith of the people. They now seek to create that faith to begin with.

These four central categories of inquiry: holy way of life, holy man, holy people, holy faith, all reveal a single fact, and that is, American Judaism, in all its forms, is vastly different from the classical Judaism that preceded it in Eastern and Central Europe, and that continues to exist in the State of Israel.

Now one must ask, what is the meaning of the changes in Judaism? How shall we interpret the materials before us? Is American Judaism the disorganized remnant of a tradition once integrated, now in a shambles, degenerate and hopeless of reformation and reconstruction, at best capable of survival like a fossil? Or do we discern something fundamentally different from its antecedents, not decayed but regenerate, the courageous response of a vital people to the new and challenging situation of modernity?

The answer depends not upon facts, on which all may agree, but on the interpretation of facts, on judgment. For American Judaism sharply poses the enigma of religion in postarchaic times: what do we understand by "religion" after the collapse of classical myth and the end of old modes of believing? If the old stands firm as stern judge of all to follow, then the verdict is clear. But if what is different may legitimately claim both to be new and possess its own integrity, then who, but the future, is to say what is decayed, or what is regenerate?

Modern people, among them Jews, sentimentally speak of sacred revelation, but they live by secular enlightenment. They speak of the voice of God, through revealed Torah guiding every action from Heaven, lending supernatural significance to trivial, commonplace matters. But they live by simple rules of accepted conduct. They read the works of prophecy, but discover knowledge through research. They fantasize about the *shtetl*, the ideal cathectic life of the corporate community. But by choice they live in the great, anomic cities of America. They profess a parochial culture and prefer endogamy. But they stand in the vanguard of international culture, in which appeals to singular revelation carry less weight than the demands of reason, and by which parochialism and self-verifying realms of discourse and meaning are set aside in favor of a single, universal language of rational thought and technology.

Clearly, what happens to archaic religious forms in modern times reveals change, and not all change is for the better. But the real problem is: what do those changes tell us about the condition of modern people, the challenges that confront them and their responses?

Concerning American Jews, the evidence before us raises the question of whether they are at all what they profess: a religious group. Half a century ago they would not have claimed "religious" as an appropriate adjective for their community. Today they insist upon it. The moralists' criticism of religion will always render ever more remote what is meant by "true religion," so we need not be detained by irrelevant and carping questions. But can there be religion with so minimal a quotient of religious experience, theological conviction, and evocative ritual, including prayer, as revealed in American Judaism? If one draws the dividing line between belief in a supernatural God and atheism, then much of American Jewry, also much of American Judaism, may have to stand on the far side of that line. If the dividing line is, in the words of Krister Stendahl, "between the closed mind and spiritual sensibility and imagination," then I contend American Jews and American Judaism may well stand within the frontier of the religious, the sacred.

Let us begin with the substitution of organizations and group activity for a holy way of life lived by each and every individual. What the Jews have done in their revision of the holy way is to conform to, in their own way to embody, the American talent at actually accomplishing things. Americans organize. They do so not to keep themselves busy, but to accomplish efficiently and with an economy of effort a great many commendable goals. They hire "professionals" to do well what most individuals cannot do at all: heal the sick, care for the needy, tend the distressed at home and far away. In modern society people do not keep guns in their homes for self-protection; they have police. Nations do not rely upon the uncertain response of well-meaning volunteers; they form armies. The things American Jews seek to accomplish their vast organizational life derive from their tradition: they want to educate the young and old, to contribute to the building of the ancient land, to see to it that prayers are said and holidays observed. Now, hiring a religious virtuoso may seem less commendable than saying one's own prayers, but it is merely an extension to ritual life of specialization people take for granted elsewhere.

In archaic times people believed that salvation depended upon keeping to the holy way, so each person kept to it, made himself sufficiently expert to know how to carry out the law. Today few believe that supernatural salvation inheres in prayers, dietary taboos, and Sabbath observances. It is therefore curious that the Jews nonetheless want to preserve the old salvific forms and symbols, as they certainly do. Few pray. Fewer still believe in prayer. It is astonishing that the synagogues persist in focusing their collective life upon liturgical functions. Perhaps the best analogy is to a museum, in which old art is preserved and displayed, though people do not paint that way any more, may not even comprehend what the painter did, or the technical obstacles he overcame. The synagogue is a living museum and preserves the liturgical and ritual life of the old tradition. Why should Jews choose this way, when earlier in their American experience they seemed to move in a different direction? Is it nostalgia for a remembered, but unavailable, experience of the sacred? Is the religious self-definition they have adopted merely an accommodation to American expectations? Or do they hope the archaic and even the supernatural may continue to speak to them?

The figure of the rabbi calls forth the same wonderment. Why call oneself "rabbi" at all, of one is not a saint, a scholar, a judge? Given the ultimate mark of secularization—the complaint that rabbis no longer reach to high places in the Jewish community— should we not ask: what is still sacred in the rabbi and his learning, calling, leadership? The answer would be "nothing whatsoever," were it not for the testimony of people's relationships to the rabbi, their fantastic expectations of him. The absurd, pathetic, posturing rabbi, without adequate education for his task, unsure of his role, at once self-isolated and complaining of his loneliness—whatever he is, he is the rabbi. He knows it. The people know it. They look to him as a kind of holy man. No nostalgia here: the rabbi is a completely American adaptation of the ancient rabbinic role.

But American society never imposed the peculiar, mainly secular definition of "Jewish clergyman" upon the modern rabbi. For two hundred years American Jewry had no rabbis at all. And the rabbis they now have are not mere Judaic versions of Protestant ministers or Roman Catholic priests, but uniquely Judaic, as much as they are exceptionally American. The remembrance of rabbis of past times—of the saints, scholars and holy men of Europe—hardly persists into the fourth generation and beyond.

The rabbi, profane and secular, is the only holy man they shall ever know. So on to him they fix their natural, human fantasies about men set apart by and for God.

The holy people, "Israel," of times past has become "the American Jewish community," uncertain what is Jewish about itself, still more unsure of what "Jewish" ought to mean at all. Surely the lingering crisis of self-definition, characteristic of modern men in many situations, marks the Jew as utterly modern and secular. Add to that the second component of the self-understanding of the holy people: concern for what the gentiles think of the Jews and readiness to admit that opinion into the Jewish assessment of the Jews. This submission to universal opinions and values hardly characterizes a holy people, set apart from all others. Frail and uncomfortable, hating those "Jewish traits" in oneself that set Jews apart from everyone else, and wanting to be Jewish—but not too much, not so much that Jews cannot *also* be undifferentiated Americans—is this the holy people that traversed thirty-five centuries of human history, proud, tenacious, alone? Can such people as these, unable to agree on anything, be called a people? Can they claim their collectivity to be holy, separate, and apart?

Surely in the passage from the sacred to the secular, the holy people has disintegrated, become a random group of discrete, scarcely similar individuals. Yet while that may seem to be so, the one point Jews affirm is that they shall be Jews. This they have in common. And their affirmation comes with such an intensity, a spiritual force, that one wonders what can be its source? A random collection of people, with merely memories in common (and that seems to me spurious sentimentality at best), or who suppose they share a common fate (which is rare), or imagine and fear a common tragedy (which is meretricious)—such a group ought not pugnaciously to affirm its existence as do the Jews. The very vigor of their activity together and the commonalities of a quite discrete folk suggest that the group, once a people, is still a people. The secular separateness of the Jews, their inner awareness of being a group, their outward view of themselves as in some ways apart from others—that separateness is probably all modern men and women can hope for, socially, to approximate "the holy." The archaic "holy people" has passed from the scene. In its place stands something different in all respects but the most important: its manifest and correct claim to continue as Jews, as a separate people.

The grandchildren of Jews who would not have understood what theologians do, but persisted in an episodic, aphoristic expression of a folk faith as theology enough, not only write theology, but claim it to be Judaic. This seems to me the decisive evidence that something new has been created out of something old: contemporary American Judaism, for all its distance from the classic forms of the past, its unbelief and secularity, constitutes a fundamentally new and autonomous development, not merely the last stages in the demise of something old and now decadent. American Judaism calls forth, in the task of formulating a systematic account of its faith, the talents of people of philosophical sophistication and religious conviction, able to speak in the name, even in the words, of the classic tradition, but in a language of discourse alien to that tradition.

I argue, therefore, that American Judaism is something more than the lingering end of olden ways and myths. It is rather the effort of modern men and women to make use of archaic ways and myths for the formation of religious way of living appropriate to an unreligious time. Spiritual sensibility and, even more, imagination are the sources for the unarticulated, but entirely evident, decision of American Jews to reconstruct out of the remnants of an evocative but incongruous heritage the materials of a humanly viable, meaningful community life. To have attempted the reconstitution of traditional villages in the metropolis and of archaic ways of seeing the world in the center of modernity would have been to deny the human value and pertinence of the tradition itself. But few wanted even to try. In the end the effort would have had no meaning. The Jews had the courage to insist life—their life together—must have more than ordinary meaning. In American Judaism they embarked upon the uncertain quest to find that meaning. Despite their failures, the gross, grotesque form they have imposed upon the old tradition, that uncommon, courageous effort seems to me to testify to whatever is good and enduring in modernity. But whether good or not, abiding or ephemeral, all that modern men and women have, and all that they shall ever have, is the mature hope to persist in that quest for meaning beyond the broken myths of old.

Yet, despite this essentially affirmative assessment, I still must ask: are American Jews a religious group? Is American Judaism a religion? No one denies that the Jews are a group, a well-demarcated ethnic community. But is the persistence, among such disproportionately small numbers of Jewry, of a religious perspective upon themselves and upon life sufficient to characterize the Jews as a religious group? The process of modernization has not merely rendered their group life more complex and varied, but also seems to have obliterated from their group life the last remnants of a religious way of viewing reality.

Many have lost sight of the full implications of the religious language and symbolism of the classic Judaic tradition. They scarcely make use of religious symbols as the way in which they as human beings and Jews relate themselves to the conditions of their existence. Such symbols as do survive scarcely relate to the conditions of group, much less of individual, existence. American Jews cannot claim to apprehend the symbolic or mythic structure of traditional Judaism or of its modern developments in the way Robert Bellah suggests (*Beyond Belief* [N.Y.: Harper and Row, 1970]): "Through religious symbols man has symbolized to himself his own identity and the order of existence in terms of which his identity makes sense." If one substitutes "Jewishness" for "religious symbols," then we have no discontinuity, for American Jews in the main do identify themselves in large measure through "being Jewish." But since the substance of "Jewishness" contains little of transcendent meaning, can it be regarded as other than of merely cultural and sociological, but not religious, interest?

Where is the human anguish, joy, tragedy, humor, mystery, wonder—in American Judaism? Where the sense of the sacred? Where the vision? Wilfred C. Smith says, "A religious symbol is successful if men can express in terms of it the highest and deepest vision of which they are capable, and if in terms of it that vision can be nourished and can be conveyed to others within one's group." Do American Jews possess such symbols, profess such a faith as to lead to a vision beyond the mundane data of their very worldly group life? That seems to me the central dilemma facing American Judaism: its commitment to the rationality, respectability, and worldliness of middle class life to which Jews aspire, and in large part have achieved, seems to conflict with the vision contained in the holy books and deeds, indeed, with the whole symbolic structure of the Judaic inheritance. When the theologians have had their say, they still have not drawn the transcendent thorn from the rational rose—and transcendence seems the prerequisite, in some form or other, of the religious quest for meaning.

Perhaps Judaism, therefore, is actually dysfunctional because both its classic and its contemporary forms (and they really are not so far apart) may not provide a secure stable foundation for the collective life of the American Jews. In so far as the Jews build that life upon solely this-worldly considerations, they render religious expression either irrelevant, or meretricious, or merely sentimental. But as soon as they speak of themselves in mythic language and respond to the existential challenge in accord with the Judaic response, they repudiate the worldliness, the confidence, the practicality of their present group life, for they thereby abandon their pugnacious secularity.

Which, then: ethnic group or religious community? If the former, why? If the latter, how? Individuals in the ethnic group are bound to raise religious questions, and if the answers do not come from Judaism, they will come from somewhere else—and this the ethnic group cannot endure. The religious community, however, is bound to exclude some in its commitment to a vision and symbolic structure, and the Jews have been wise in not excluding anyone, whatever his vision, born into their group.

This disintegration of the archaic religious and ethnic unity of the "holy people" seems to me the most important Jewish testimony about what it means to be modern. But the story of the tension between the ethnic datum of Jewish group life and the religious critique and interpretation of that group life forms the substance of the history of Judaism. If so, the modern age brings new evidence of an astonishing continuity.

4

Assimilation and Self-Hatred in Modern Jewish Life

Assimilation denotes the reception of aliens by a host-society and the aliens' gradual acceptance of the traits of that host-culture. The history of the Jewish people is the story of how the Jews entered into one culture after another, and came to regard their cultural acquisitions as essentially Jewish. Eastern European cuisine among American Jewry is one obvious example; Greek philosophy among Spanish Jewry is another; Roman methods of legal codification among Palestinian Jewry is a third. In all three instances Jews took over and judaized cultural traits derived from other cultures, and thereafter defended and cherished them as quintessentially Jewish. So we have stuffed derma, Maimonides, and the Mishnah. to name three examples of the assimilation through judaization of originally alien traits or creations.

The extent of the Jews' assimilation of the various cultures encountered in their history cannot be overestimated. We may not take for granted that we may find peculiarly "Jewish" approaches to intellectual life, for example. Some people suppose that talmudic dialectic is uniquely Jewish. The dialectic, however, is formed of Roman principles of legal codification and Greek principles of rhetoric. The Jewish academies of late antiquity certainly are similar to Christian monastaries of the same time and place. Although a discipline may be peculiar to a tradition of learning and still be derivative, I doubt that Jewish learning can be associated over a long period of time with any particular discipline. The Jews can lay no persuasive claim to exclusive possession of subtlety or cleverness, devotion to the intellectual life, dedication to matters of the spirit, or any of the other traits, pejorative or complimentary, claimed for them by their religious and secular enemies or apologists.

In the early days of Reform Judaism, it was thought that if we uncover the "origin" of a practice or belief, we may then decide whether it is "essential" or peripheral. Nowadays we see less interest in questions of origins. The exposure of the genetic fallacy may have been part of the reason for this shift. We recognize that determination of the origin does not exhaust the meanings of beliefs or practices. Yet there is another source for this dwindling of interest. For it has become progressively more difficult, with the advance of scholarship, to discover any deeply "Jewish" or "Judaic" practice which was not in some degree the creation of another culture or civilization.

The Jewish calender, that "unique" construction of Judaism, derives mostly from the Canaanites. One may argue that the festivals were "monotheized" or "judaized." But, in fact, different verbal explanations have been imposed on the same festivals celebrating the same natural phenomena of the same Palestinian agricultural year. The Jews, over long centuries, have assumed as their own what was produced originally by others. Their infinite adaptability has been made possible by short memories and by tenacious insistence on the Jewish origins of purely gentile or pagan customs. Whatever was or was not Jewish, a great many things have *become* so. Jewishness thus is not static but dynamic, and assimilation is the source of the dynamism.

It is clear, therefore, that the history of Judaism is also the history of the assimilation by the Jews of the cultural, social, and religious traits characteristic of their neighbors. How shall we evaluate that phenomenon? Here I advance the view of Gerson D. Cohen ("The Blessing of Assimilation in Jewish History," *Commencement Address,* June 1966, Hebrew Teachers College, Boston):

> A frank appraisal of the periods of great Jewish creativity will indicate that not only did a certain amount of assimilation and acculturation *not* impede Jewish continuity and creativity, but that, in a profound sense, this assimilation or acculturation was even a stimulus to original thinking and expression and, con-

sequently, a source of renewed vitality. To a considerable degree the Jews survived as a vital group ... because they changed their names, their language, their clothing, and with them, some of their patterns of thought and expression. This ability to translate, to readapt and reorient themselves to new situations, while retaining a basic inner core of continuity, was largely responsible, if not for their survival, at least for their vitality.

Cohen points out, to be sure, that people on the fringe preferred to identify with the majority group. This occasionally happened. But, Cohen stresses, "We Jews have always been and will doubtless continue to be a minority group. Now a minority that does not wish to ghettoize itself, one that refuses to become fossilized, will inevitably have to acculturate itself, i.e., to assimilate at least to some extent." Assimilation is a fact of Jewish life and, on the whole, it has been a fact Jews may accept with optimism.

As Cohen stresses, Jews confront the problem of assimilation in two ways. One is to withdraw. The other is to utilize assimilation for a new source of vitality. Cohen cites Ahad Ha'Am, who distinguished between *ḥiqqui shel hitḥarut* and *ḥiqqui shel hitbolelut*—imitation stimulated by the challenge of new ideas and imitation motivated by the desire to be absorbed. Cohen advances this notion:

I would ... rather speak of the healthy appropriation of new forms and ideas for the sake of our *own* growth and enrichment. Assimilation ... can become a kind of blessing, for assimilation bears within it a certain seminal power which serves as a challenge and a goad to renewed creativity. The great ages of Jewish creativity ... have always been products of the challenge of assimilation and of the response of leaders, who were to a certain extent assimilated themselves.

Following Cohen, Jews need not regard the assimilation of Jewry into Western civilization as disheartening or threatening. They ought, rather, to see it as an invigorating and challenging situation.

Nor should one suppose that the State of Israel is exempt from the assimilative situation of Diaspora Jewry. Israel uses Hebrew to farm in the modern mode, to manufacture for the world market, to think in a wholly contemporary fashion about the great issues facing the modern world, to make war according to the requirements of modern technology. Israeli Jews do not differ from Western Jews; both have adopted the international culture—music, art, literature, philosophy—of Western Europe and North America. There is no place to hide from the transistor radio. No one wants to "escape" from modern medicine. No ghetto is immune from the healthy virus of modernity.

Let us now turn to one of the unwanted consequences of the movement of Jewry from an isolated culture into international civilization. In the past, the Jews lived well insulated from the opinions of gentiles. Their social setting tended to separate them, and their theological conviction rendered them indifferent to what the gentiles had to say about them. Jews not only knew they were different from others, but regarded those differences as a matter of destiny. The statement in the *Alenu* prayer, "Who has not made us like the gentiles," was a matter of thanksgiving, pride, and joy, a self-conscious articulation of Israel's unique peoplehood. The myth of peoplehood transformed difference into destiny.

In modern times, however, assimilation, formerly unconscious and unplanned, became both a public program and a personal policy. The Jews determined that they should live not only among gentiles, but with them. They would share their way of living, their cultural, social, and economic life and values. In one respect only would they differ: in matters of religion, meaning chiefly questions of faith—and these were not important. This reversal of traditional attitudes was espoused not only by Reform Judaism in Germany, but also by modern Orthodox leaders such as Samson R. Hirsch, who taught that Jews could be both good Germans and strictly traditional Jews, read both Goethe and Talmud. Orthodoxy differed from Reform in its order of priorities: the Torah would stand as the criterion of modernity, and not the reverse.

But before Jews, whether Reform or Orthodox, could conceive of themselves in such a new situation, they had to affirm modern culture in a way in which they never accepted or affirmed the cultures of ancient and medieval times. The assimilation of ancient and medieval cultures had come about naturally and quietly. It had not challenged the beliefs and practices Jews regarded as eternal and unchanging, but had allowed those beliefs and practices to continue with renewed vigor. Modern assimilation, however, held as a deliberate and positive goal the dejudaization of the Jews.

Now for the first time in centuries Jews took to heart what gentiles said about them. And since the European Jews lived in an age of virulent anti-Semitism, most of what gentiles had to say was derogatory. The "right" regarded the Jews as agents of change and therefore hated them; the "left" differed—it hated only what was *Jewish* about the Jews. Liberals argued that allowing Jews to enter into the common life of European politics and culture would hasten their dejudaization. So the Jewish problem resolved itself into a debate on how to rid Europe of Jews and Judaism.

One result was the Zionist movement, which accepted the premises of European anti-Semitism, and held that the only solution to the Jewish problem was the creation of a Jewish state, which would "normalize" the character of the Jewish people. That is to say, Zionism proposed to make the Jews like the gentiles. Another result was Reform Judaism, which also accepted the premises of European anti-Semitism, and held that the only solution was to limit the differences between Jews and gentiles to matters of religious belief. Reforming Jewish tradition would permit Jews to become more like their neighbors. Individual Jews reacted in still a third way—and it was profoundly tragic. They responded to the hatred of gentiles by hating themselves as Jews, by hating those traits the gentiles thought to be particularly Jewish.

European Jewish self-hatred was pathological, producing psychosis and occasionally leading to suicide. But by and large this sickness remained outside of Jewish institutions and leadership strata, for those infected by self-hatred fled the Jewish community. The most profound analysis of European Jewry's self-hatred is found in Theodor Lessing's *Der Jüdische Selbsthass* (Berlin, 1930). Lessing himself was a sad man, who lived a life of self-hatred. He was murdered on August 31, 1933, in Marienbad, by three Sudeten German-Czech Nazis who were paid 80,000 marks for the deed by Goering. Lessing stresses that the Jews of Europe wonder, "Why does no one love us?" And they answer, "Because we are at fault." Lessing sees this as a contemporary psychological counterpart to the traditional theology of disaster: "Because of our sins, we have been exiled from our land."

Lessing tells the story of six European Jewish intellectuals, most of whom ended as suicides. One wrote as follows:

I force myself not to think about it. But what does it help?—It thinks within me, it thinks of itself, it does not ask about my wish and will and the natural urge to flee from what is painful, ugly, deadly. It is there, all the time, it is within me: this knowledge about my descent. Just as a leper or a person sick with cancer carries his repulsive disease hidden under his dress and yet knows about it himself every moment, so I carry the shame and disgrace, the metaphysical guilt of my being a Jew.
What are all the sufferings and disappointments and inhibitions which come from outside in comparison with this hell within? To have to be what one despises!... Because here all rationalizations, all attempts to cover up, all desire to lie to oneself, all this is useless here. It is quite clear to me, ruthlessly clear: Jewishness lies in existence. You cannot shake it off. Just as little as a dog or a pig can shake off its being a dog or its being a pig, just so little do I tear myself, my own self, away from the eternal ties of existence, which hold me on that step between man and animal: the Jews.

The closing passage is without parallel even in the pathological literature of Jewish self-hatred:

There exists today hardly a more tragic fate than that of those few who have truly fought themselves free from their Jewish ancestry and who now discovered that people do not believe them, do not want to believe them. Where, where can we go? Behind us lie revulsion and disgust, in front of us yawns an abyss.... Nameless, rootless. Mercilessly exiled into a circle of hatred rigid with death.... And I feel as if I had to carry on my shoulders the entire accumulated guilt of that cursed breed of men whose poisonous elf-blood is becoming my virus. I feel as if I, I alone, had to do penance for every crime those people are committing against German-ness....
And to the Germans I should like to shout: Remain hard! Remain hard! Have no mercy! Not even with me!
Germans, your walls must remain secure against penetration. They must not have any secret little door in the rear which could be opened for single persons. Because, surely, some day through this little door treason would creep in.... Close your hearts and your ears to all those who from out there still beg for admission. Everything is at stake! You last little fortress of Aryanism, remain strong and faithful!

No, no, no—it was not just that God wanted to spare Sodom
and Gomorra because of one righteous man! Not even for the
sake of ten, not for the sake of a hundred righteous men.
Away with this pestilential poor! Burn out this nest of wasps!
Even though along with the unrighteous a hundred righteous
ones are destroyed. What do they matter? What do we matter?
What do I matter? No! Have no mercy! I beg of you.

Self-hatred is not unique to Jews. It is an element in every
human personality. All must fight the conflict between self-
esteem and self-hatred. Self-esteem begins in earliest childhood.
Eric Erikson writes somewhere, "Through the coincidence of
physical mastery and cultural meaning, of functional pleasure and
social recognition, one achieves a realistic self-esteem." Children
naturally begin with self-love, but it must be corroborated by
experience which gives them the feeling that they fulfill their own
ego-ideals. Erikson stresses that there must be tangible social
recognition, "a feeling of continued communal meaning," in
order for the adolescent to develop a mature sense of self-esteem.

But the Jewish children in Europe and in North America face
discontinuity between what they learn in childhood and at home,
on the one side, and continued communal meaning, on the other.
At home they learn that they are Jews. What they learn about the
meaning of that fact will vary. In some few homes, being Jewish is
a source of joy and endless pleasures; in many others, it is merely
a social datum. But the fact of Jewishness contains within itself
no pleasures or joys, no larger meaning, nothing of communal or
theological significance.

And it contradicts a communal fact that the child perceives
quite early: not everyone is Jewish. Most people are something
else. The child rapidly senses that being Jewish is "different."
Being Jewish, therefore, stands as an obstacle to the child's
growth. The cultural meaning of the home conflicts with the social
recognition achieved outside of the home. The Jewish child's
self-love is *not* corroborated by experience—for the child cannot
expect an opportunity to employ what is learned in the Jewish
experiences of childhood and to acquire thereby a feeling of continued communal meaning.

Now add to the fact that Jewish children find themselves different the fact that the gentile world openly or insidiously tells them
the "Jewish-difference" is a bad one. The majority is not only

different, but better—for, after all, the world celebrates Christmas, but only some Jews celebrate Hanukkah. The psychological consequences, in terms of Erikson's analysis, will be obvious. Jewish children will sense a deep discontinuity, and will see themselves as inferior, different, and bad because of the difference. If the Jewish child attends a public school, this awareness cannot be postponed beyond the second or third grade, a period in which the earliest psychological conflicts are by and large dormant. At that age the male child may continue to compare himself with his father; this comparison may arouse a sense of guilt and of inferiority. Now the religion of the father enters the picture: the family is Jewish. Being Jewish is being different. Being Jewish is not as good as being gentile. The father, toward whom guilt is already present, is Jewish and made the child. The normal guilt of the earliest school years may thus turn into hatred of the father—or it may produce hatred of the self as a surrogate for hatred of the father.

Let us bring together the two approaches to the problem of Jewish self-hatred. Lessing tells us that the culture and religion of the Jews taught them over the centuries to blame themselves for their own misfortunes. Erikson tells us that the personality development of each child is apt to produce severe psychological problems if self-esteem cannot be fully established in the earliest years through communal as well as familial support. Jewish children in the Western communities experience being a minority and being different from people one admires. The response is cultural and historical, on the one side, and psychological and personal, on the other. And the inevitable union of history and culture with psychology and personality-development cannot be postponed; the one supplies explanations for the experiences produced by the other.

If we look for pathological cases of Jewish self-hatred among North American Jewry, we should easily find them. But on the whole, self-hatred takes a different form here. It is merely neurotic, but it is not limited to individuals. It characterizes the community as a whole, and is reflected in the Jewish community's commitment to nonsectarianism, and in its niggardly support for the cultural, scholarly, and religious programs and institutions that make Jews Jewish.

How to account for the difference? I think the obvious answer is that on the whole Jews in the United States and Canada enjoy an enviable status in economic, social, cultural, and political life. Anti-Semitism does not take the virulent and destructive forms it did in Western Europe before World War II. We have no anti-Semitic political parties; universities are, on the whole, open to Jews, most professions accept Jews; discrimination in the executive suite and in upper-class social clubs by and large constitutes a form of social snobbery, not an ideology of race and culture. American and Canadian societies in the balance are not racist. But these facts cannot change the situation of the *Galut:* the Jews are still a minority, still correctly see themselves as different from the majority. Those differences still add up to abnormality.

Part Two

Response to Freedom I
The Place of "The Holocaust" in American Judaism

Introduction

Now that we have considered the critical challenges to the imagination and self-understanding of Jews in American, we turn to examine the principal components in their mythic life, the symbols they evoke to explain to themselves the meaning of their distinctive existence as a group and of their individual participation in that group. These are two. First, there is the matter of "the Holocaust," certainly the center of Judaic public discourse in America and the source of self-evident truths. Second, there is the "redemption" contained in the creation of maintenance of the State of Israel. Together this "myth of Holocaust and redemption" makes sense to the American Jew of why he or she is Jewish and explains that world in which "being Jewish" takes place. In this way the challenge of explaining why, in a free society, a person should be part of the Jewish people, and what it means to take part in the life of that distinctive social group, is met. But more important, the implicit meaning of life as part of that group (for people do not make choices, but they reflect on the consequences of choices for themselves already made by others and by society) is worked out. The negative meaning of "being Jewish" is carried to its extreme in the fully realized potentialities of the extermination of European Jewry, now turned into a cosmic truth under the title, "the Holocaust." The affirmative meaning of "being Jewish" cannot be understood, within the framework of the present mythic structure, outside of the negative, and vice versa. So we begin with the matter of the place of "the Holocaust" in the symbolic structure of contemporary American Judaism.

The issue of the destruction of European Jewry is not theological but psychological and social: why does "the Holocaust" presently play so provocative a role in the imaginative and social life of American Judaism, and what does the importance accorded to that corpus of symbols and stories reveal to us about the character of American Judaism and Jews? The three papers in this part explore that question. They may scarcely be said to complete the inquiry. What they contribute is little more than clearing away some debris. The first and most important contribution made here is to point out that, from the viewpoint of the established theological power of Judaism, the extermination of European Jewry in no way asks afresh but only with renewed urgency the old and, alas, familiar question of theodicy. The established question remains, in all its awesome mystery, essentially unchanged, fundamentally no more, no less, relevant than it always was. The necessary consequence of that obvious statement is that "the Holocaust" is not an inevitable outcome of theological reflection on the meaning of the extermination of European Jewry. Indeed, why that event should have become the focus of public discourse in Judaism at just the time it did, and among just the people for whom it serves as a generative source of symbols and myths, seems to me the first and most important question. The framing of the question in these terms—why here? why now? why us?—is the second contribution offered by these papers.

The first paper here is the important one. By restating what I believe to be the salvific myth framed by those who deem the destruction of European Jewry to be "the Holocaust," I suggest why that symbol of "Holocaust" takes the critical place accorded to it in normative American Judaism. The fundamental reason is that anti-Semitism is not something people confront only when they read books about the destruction of European Jewry. It is personal and real, something they remember and recognize in their own life. The extermination of European Jewry stands at the end of a continuum, on the other end of which American Jews stand and know they stand. The pertinence of the events, their availability for mythicization and theologization (so to speak)—these are the consequence of their being perfectly within the range of both imagination and social experience.

But there is that other side, the side of redemption, which makes it possible to contemplate the horror and to make use of it in the formation of a viable understanding of Judaic existence. Without Zionism, "the Holocaust" is unbearable and to be avoided, except as a topic for learned books about unspeakable facts. The myth of "the Holocaust" is complete only in the redemption of the Jewish nation, the state of Jewish existence called the State of Israel. The point at which the myth of "Holocaust and redemption" becomes compelling is the moment at which the redemption appears to be credible, not 1948 (for most) or even the 1950s (for many), but 1967.

At that point, too, I argue, "the Holocaust" became a Jewish idiomatic way of expressing what pretty much everyone wanted to say in some formulation or other. So at this point at which conversation among Jews appears to be the most distinctively Judaic, it is claimed here, we discern the most subtle, therefore striking, evidence of completed acculturation, indeed assimilation, to which reference was made in the first part. The second paper here, "How the Extermination of European Jewry Became 'the Holocaust,'" reenforces the argument of the first that "the Holocaust" became a pervasive theme of Judaic discourse not in the decades following the end of the war, but much later on.

The issue of why "the Holocaust" came to the fore when it did and not earlier, and the distinctively American, rather commonplace, ways in which "the Holocaust" was made into a source of slogans and attitudes alike, is raised once more. The advance in the argument comes in my recognition, by 1979, of what I did not perceive in 1972, that "the Holocaust" was turning out to define a significant sector of that "civil religion" of American Jews which here is deemed American Judaism. The recognition that to Israeli civil religion the extermination of European Jewry provides a natural and fundamental component I owe to Charles Liebman, who has spelled this matter out in conversation and in writing. The curiously dysfunctional aspect of the same thing in this country is my point. What I find difficult to explain is how the "lessons of the Holocaust" can be learned by people who, if the lessons uniformly set forth are taken seriously, must no longer trust their neighbors. What sort of civil religion makes sense when its ultimate effect is to create distrust and disbelief I cannot say. But the place of "the Holocaust" in American Judaism seems to me considerably less dysfunctional than, on the surface, it appears to be. It is only the consequence drawn from the contemplation of the myth that are somewhat awry.

The final paper here, "Jubilee in Tübingen," is more personal. It is meant to express the simple point in the closing sentence: there really was a holocaust. And there is no need, except when we speak of an evocative myth, bearing its own predictable consequences of ideology and ritual, to add quotation marks or to capitalize the h. When this paper originally was printed, the final sentence in error had Holocaust. But there really was a holocaust.

5

The Implications of "The Holocaust"

The events of 1933–48 constitute one of the decisve moments in the history of Judaism, to be compared in their far-reaching effects to the destruction of the First and Second Temples, 586 B.C. and A.D. 70; the massacre of Rhineland Jewries, 1096; the aftermath of the Black Plague, 1349; the expulsion of the Jews from Spain, 1492; or the Ukrainian massacres of 1648–49. But while after the latter disasters the Jews responded in essentially religious ways, the response the Holocaust and the creation of the State of Israel on the surface has not been religious. That is to say, while in the past people explained disaster as a result of sin and therefore sought means of reconciliation with God and atonement for sin, in the twentieth century the Jews superficially did not. Instead they have done what seem secular, and not religious, deeds; they raised money, engaged in political action, and did all the other things modern, secular people, confident they can cope with anything, normally do. They did not write new prayers or holy books, create new theologies, or develop new religious ideas and institutions.

Yet I should argue that the response to the Holocaust and the creation of the State of Israel differs in form, but not in substance, from earlier responses to disaster. The form now is secular. The substance is deeply religious. For the effect of the Holocaust and the creation of the State of Israel on the Jews is to produce a new myth—by myth I mean a transcendent perspective on events, a story lending meaning and imparting sanctity to ordinary, every-day actions—and a new religious affirmation.

Let me recount the salvific story as it is nearly universally perceived by the senior generation of American Jews—those who came to maturity before 1945:

Once upon a time, when I was a young man, I felt helpless before the world. I was a Jew, when being Jewish was a bad thing. As a child, I saw my old Jewish parents, speaking a foreign language and alien in countless ways, isolated from America. And I saw America, dimly perceived to be sure, exciting and promising, but hostile to me as a Jew. I could not get into a good college. I could not aspire to medical school. I could not become an architect or an engineer. I could not even work for an electric utility.

When I took my vacation, I could not go just anywhere, but had to ask whether Jews would be welcome, tolerated, embarrassed, or thrown out. Being Jewish was uncomfortable. Yet I could not give it up. My mother and my father had made me what I was. I could hide, but could not wholly deny, not to myself even if to others, that I was a Jew. And I could not afford the price in diminished self-esteem of opportunity denied, aspiration deferred, and insult endured. Above all, I saw myself as weak and pitiful. I could not do anything about being a Jew nor could I do much to improve my lot as a Jew.

Then came Hitler and I saw that what was my private lot was the dismal fate of every Jew. Everywhere Jew hatred was raised from the gutter to the heights. Not from Germany alone, but from people I might meet at work or in the streets I learned that being Jewish was a metaphysical evil. "The Jews" were not accepted, but debated. Friends would claim we were not all bad. Enemies said we were. And we had nothing to say at all.

As I approached maturity, a still more frightening fact confronted me. People guilty of no crime but Jewish birth were forced to flee their homeland, and no one would accept them. Ships filled with ordinary men, women, and children searched the oceans for a safe harbor. And I and they had nothing in common but one fact, and that fact made all else inconsequential. Had I been there, I should have been among them. I too, should not have been saved at the sea.

Then came the war and, in its aftermath, the revelation of the shame and horror of holocaust, the decay and corrosive hopelessness of the DP camps, the contempt of the nations, who would neither accept nor help the saved remnants of hell.

At the darkest hour came the dawn. The State of Israel saved the remnant and gave meaning and significance to the inferno. After the dawn, the great light: Jews no longer helpless, weak, unable to decide their own fate, but strong, confident, decisive.

And then came the corrupting doubt: if I were there, I should have died in hell, But now has come redemption and I am here, not there.

How much security in knowing that if it should happen again I shall not be lost. But how great a debt paid in guilt for being where I am and who I am!

This story of mine tells the myth that gives meaning and transcendence to the petty lives of ordinary people—the myth of the darkness follwed by light, of passage though the netherworld and past the gates of hell, then, purified by suffering and by blood, into the new age. The naturalist myth of American Jewry—it is not the leaders' alone—conforms to the supernatural structure of the classic myths of salvific religions from time immemorial. And well it might, for a salvific myth has to tell the story of sin and redemption, disaster and salvation, the old being and the new, the vanquishing of death and mourning, crying and pain, the passing away of former things. The vision of the new Jerusalem, complete in 1967, beckoned not tourists, but pilgrims to the new heaven and the new earth. This, as I said, is the myth that shapes the mind and imagination of American Jewry, supplies the correct interpretation and denotes the true significance of everyday events, and turns workaday people into saints. This is the myth that transforms commonplace affairs into history, makes writing a check into a sacred act.

It is not faith, theology, ideology—for none offers reasons for its soundness, or needs to. It is myth in that it so closely corresponds to, and yet so magically transforms and elevates, reality that people take vision and interpretation for fact. They do not need to believe in or affirm the myth, for they know it to be true. In that they are confident of the exact correspondence between reality and the story that explains reality, they are the saved, the saints, the witnesses to the end of days. We know this is how things really were and what they really meant. We know it because the myth of suffering and redemption corresponds to our perceptions of reality, evokes immediate recognition and assent.

It not only bears meaning, it imparts meaning precisely because it explains experience and derives from what we know to be true.

But one must ask whether experience is so stable, the world so unchanging, that we may continue to explain today's reality in terms of what happened yesterday. The answer is that, much as we might want to, we cannot. The world has moved on. We can remember, but we cannot reenact what happened. We cannot replicate the experiences which required explanation according to a profound account of the human and the Jewish condition. We cannot, because our children will not allow it. They experience a different world—perhaps not better, perhaps not so simple, but certainly different. They know about events, but have not experienced them. And what they know they perceive through their experience of a very different world. The story that gives meaning and imparts transcendence to the everyday experiences of being Jewish simply does not correspond to the reality of the generations born since 1945. They did not know the frightful insecurity, did not face the meaninglessness of Jewish suffering, therefore cannot appreciate the salvation that dawned with the creation of the State of Israel.

Theirs is a more complicated world. Not for them the simple choice of death or life, the simple encounter with uncomplicated evil. For them Jewishness also is more complicated, for while the world of the 1930s and 1940s imparted a "Jewish education," and a "Jewish consciousness" was elicited by reading a newspaper or simply encountering a hostile society, today's world does not constitute a school without walls for the education of the Jews. That is, I think, a good thing. Being Jewish no longer is imposed by negative experiences but now is called forth by affirmative ones. For the younger generation the State of Israel stands not as the end of despair but as the beginning of hope. It enriches the choices facing the young Jew and expands his consciousness of the potentialities of Jewishness. Not its existence, but its complexity, is important. Not its perfection but its imperfection is compelling. It is important as the object not of fantasy, but of perceived reality.

The effect of the Holocaust on Jewish psychology today has to be regarded as ambiguous and equivocal because we deal with two quite separate generations. The first is the one which lived through the frightening, sichkening events of the decade and a half of Hitler. The second is the one which has not. In my view the new generations—those born since 1945—have to be understood in entirely different terms from the old generations. The major difference is that the new generations are considerably healthier and, if they choose to be Jewish at all, their Jewishness is substantially more affirmative.

That is not to suggest they are less involved with the Holocaust and with the State of Israel. The contrary is the case.

The reality of the State of Israel turns out to fascinate the younger generation still more than the fantasy mesmerized the parents. If the 1950s and '60s were times in which the State of Israel rose to the top of the agendum of American Jewry, in the 1970s it seems to constitute the whole of that agendum. No other Jewish issue has the power to engage the younger generation of Jews as does the issue of the State of Israel. Anti-Zionism and anti-Israelism are virtually nonexistent among the new generation of Jews. (Those on the fringes are not interesting in the present context.) That is to say, whether or not there should be a state of Israel, why there should be such a state, how one must justify the existence of a Jewish state in terms of a higher morality or claim in its behalf that it is a light to the nations—these modes of thought are simply alien. The State of Israel *is*. The issue for the younger generation is not: is it a good thing or a bad thing? The issue is: since we know no other world but one in which the State of Israel is present, how shall we relate to the important part of the world in which we live?

The younger generation exhibits a healthier relationship to the State of Israel than did its parents, not because it is more virtuous (despite its fantasies), but because it has not had to live through the frightening, sickening experiences of those parents. If the myth of the fathers and mothers is irrelevant to the children, and if the fantasy-ridden relationships of the parents are not replicated by the children, the reason is that the young people have grown up in a healthier world. It is a world not without its nightmares, but with different, less terrifying nightmares for the Jews in particular. In days gone by, the "Jewish problem" belonged to Jews alone. Whether we lived or died was our problem. But now the problem of life or death faces all mankind; we are no longer singled out for extermination. The terror is everyone's. If there is a just God, a mark of his justice is that those who did not share our anguish must now share our nightmares—an exact, if slow, measure of justice. We who saw ourselves all alone in the death camps have been joined by the rest of the world. Next time fire instead of gas, perhaps. But meanwhile it is an easier life.

Nor should we ignore the fact that for the younger generation being Jewish has conferred the practical advantages of a group capable of mutual protection in a generally undifferentiated society. It has been a positive advantage in the recent past. Add to this the devotion of the Jewish parent to the Jewish child. Jewish children are treated in Jewish homes as very special beings. This makes young Jews strive to excel in the rest of society as they did at home. To be sure, this produces a large crop of Jewish adults who blame their Jewishness for the fact that the rest of society does not treat them as did their parents. These are people who need evidence to explain what they see as their own failure, which is actually explicable their own impossible demands on themselves and on society. Being Jewish in the recent past in the balance has been an advantage rather than a disability. The younger generation is better off on that account.

To summarize: the generations that liven through disaster and triumph, darkness and light, understand the world in terms of a salvific myth. The generations that have merely heard about the darkness but have daily lived in the light take for granted the very redemption that lies at the heart of the salvific myth. The psychological consequences for the one should be different from those for the other. In theory, at least, the effects of the Holocaust on those who went through it, either in the flesh or in the spirit, have been sickening. The survivors will have a survivor mentality; they will see the world as essentially hostile and will distrust, rather than trust, the outsider. They will exhibit the traits of citizens of a city under siege, feeling always threatened, always alone, always on the defensive. The new generation, which has not lived under siege, should develop greater trust in the world. They should regard the world as essentially neutral, if not friendly, and should have the capacity to trust the outsider. Yet, though the psychological experiences differ, the end result is much the same. The new generation is just as Israel-oriented as the old; if anything, it identifies still more intensely than before with the Jewish people.

The theological impact of the Holocaust and the rise of the

State of Israel normally is assessed in terms of two significant names, Richard L. Rubenstein and Emil Fackenheim. Rubenstein's response to the Holocaust has been searching and courageous. He has raised the difficult questions and responded with painful honesty. The consequence has been an unprecedented torrent of personal abuse, so that he has nearly been driven out of Jewish public life. He has been called a Nazi and compared to Hitler! The abuse to which he has been subjected seems to me the highest possible tribute on the part of his enemies to the compelling importance of his contribution. Since what he has proposed evidently is seen to be unanswerable, the theology has been ignored, but the theologian has been abused. Consequently, Rubenstein has taken the view that anyone who does not agree with his position is an "Establishment" theologian—as though American Judaism has anything like a theological "Establishment." To Rubenstein's credit, he argues with his opposition by name and in a respectful way. His most prominent critic, Emil Fackenheim, by contrast writes about a "radical" (his quotation marks—I do not know what they are supposed to mean here) Jewish theologian, but in much of his writing rarely alludes to Rubenstein by name, and when he does, it is to compare Rubenstein to Nazis, for instance, Ulrich Heidegger. This sort of onomastic homicide not only does not do credit to the magician, but also does not work. It surely is not a dignified way in which to carry on theological discourse. But perhaps dignity and autonomy are the wrong categories of criticism; in the presence of emotions bordering on hysteria even rational criticism itself is probably too rational an expectation.

What is Rubenstein's message? It has been eloquently stated in various places. I believe the most cogent expression of his viewpoint on the centrality of the Holocaust is in his contribution to *Commentary*'s Symposium on Jewish Belief, reprinted in his *After Auschwitz: Essays in Contemporary Judaism* (Indianapolis: Bobbs-Merrill, 1966):

> I believe the greatest single challenge to modern Judaism arises out of the question of God and the death camps. I am amazed at the silence of contemporary Jewish tehologians on this most crucial and agonizing of all Jewish issues. How can Jews believe in an omnipotent, beneficent God after Auschwitz? Traditional Jewish theology maintains that God is the

ultimate, omnipotent actor in the historical drama. It has interpreted every major catastrophe in Jewish history as God's
punishment of a sinful Israel. I fail to see how this position can
be maintained without regarding Hitler and the SS as in-
struments of God's will. The agony of European Jewry cannot
be likened to the testing of Job. To see any purpose in the death
camps, the traditional believer is forced to regard the most
demonic, antihuman explosion in all history as a meaningful
expression of God's purposes. The idea is simply too obscene
for me to accept. I do not think that the full impact of Auschwitz has yet been felt in Jewish theology or Jewish life.
Great religious revolutions have their own period of gestation.
No man knows the hour when the full impact of Auschwitz will
be felt, but no religious community can endure so hideous a
wounding without undergoing vast inner disorders.

Though I believe that a void stands where once we experienced God's presence, I do not think Judaism has lost its
meaning or its power. I do not believe that a theistic God is
necessary for Jewish religious life. Dietrich Bonhoeffer has
written that our problem is how to speak of God in an age of no
religion. I believe that our problem is how to speak of religion
in an age of no God. I have suggested that Judaism is the way in
which we share the decisive times and crises of life through the
traditions of our inherited community. The need for that sharing is not diminished in the time of the death of God. We no
longer believe in the God who has the power to annul the tragic
necessities of existence; the need religiously to share that
existence remains.

It should not be supposed that Rubenstein's is an essentially
destructive conclusion. On the contrary, he draws from the
Holocaust a constructive, if astringent, message:

Death and rebirth are the great moments of religious experience. In the twentieth century the Jewish phoenix has known
both: in Germany and eastern Europe, we Jews have tasted the
bitterest and the most degrading of deaths. Yet death was not
the last word. We do not pity ourselves. Death in Europe was
followed by resurrection in our ancestral home. We are free as
no men before us have ever been. Having lost everything, we
have nothing further to lose and no further fear of loss. Our
existence has in truth been a being-unto-death. We have passed
beyond all illusion and hope. We have learned in the crisis that
we were totally and nakedly alone, that we could expect neither

support nor succor from God or from our fellow creatures. No men have known as we have how truly God in His holiness slays those to whom He gives life. This has been a liberating knowledge, at least for the survivors, and all Jews everywhere regard themselves as having escaped by the skin of their teeth, whether they were born in Europe or elsewhere. We have lost all hope and faith. We have also lost all possibility of disappointment. Expecting absolutely nothing from God or man, we rejoice in whatever we receive. We have learned the nakedness of every human pretense. No people has come to know as we have how deeply man is an insubstantial nothingness before the awesome and terrible majesty of the Lord. We accept our nothingness—nay, we even rejoice in it—for in finding our nothingness we have found both ourselves and the God who alone is true substance. We did not ask to be born; we did not ask for our absurd existence in the world; nor have we asked for the fated destiny which has hung about us as Jews. Yet we would would not exchange it, nor would we deny it, for when nothing is asked for, nothing is hoped for, nothing is expected; all that we receive is truly grace.

Fackenheim's contrary view is that "Auschwitz" produces a new commandment to the Jewish people: to preserve the Jewish people and the Jewish religion. Michael Wyschogrod summarizes Fackenheim's viewpoint as follows ("Faith and the Holocaust," *Judaism* 20 [Summer 1971]):

What then, is adequate?
Only obedience to the Voice of Auschwitz. This voice, as heard by Fackenheim, commands the survival of Jews and Judaism. Because Hitler was bent upon the destruction of both, it is the duty of those Jews who survived Hitler to make sure that they do not do his work, that they do not, by assimilation, bring about the disappearance of what Hitler attempted but ultimately failed to destroy. For the religious Jew, this means that he must go on being religious, however inadequate Auschwitz has shown his frame of reference to be. And for the secular Jew, the Voice of Auschwitz commands not faith, which even the Voice of Auschwitz cannot command, but preservation of Jews and Judaism. Speaking of the significance of the Voice of Auschwitz for the secular Jew, Fackenheim writes: "No less inescapable is this Power for the secularist Jew who has all along been outside the Midrashic framework and this despite the fact that the Voice of Auschwitz does not

enable him to return into this framework. He cannot return; but neither may he turn the Voice of Auschwitz against that of Sinai. For he may not cut off his secular present from the religious past: The Voice of Auschwitz commands Jewish unity.'' The sin of Rubenstein is, therefore, that he permits Auschwitz further to divide the Jewish people at a time when survival is paramount if Hitler is not be be handed a post-humous victory, and survival demands unity. Because this is so, Rubenstein should presumably soft-pedal his doubts so as not to threaten the Jewish people at a time when everything must be secondary to the issue of survival.

What may be said in behalf of Fackenheim's argument? He has the merit of placing the Holocaust at the head of Judaic theological discourse and of doing so in such a way that the central problem is not theodicy. Rubenstein's stress on the issue of how a just God could have permitted so formidable an injustice—an understatement of the issue to be sure—leads him to the position just now outlined. Fackenheim's formulation of the issue of the Holocaust in terms of its meaning to the secular, not to the religious, Jew sidesteps the surely insoluble issue of theology and so opens a constructive and forward-looking discourse on the primary issue facing contemporary Judaism—the issue of secularity and unbelief.

Rubenstein tends, therefore, to center his interest on the tragic events themselves, while Fackenstein prefers to make those events speak to the contemporary situation of Jewry. One may compare Rubenstein's mode of thought to that of the first-century apocalyptic visionaries; Fackenheim's to that of the rabbis of the same period. After 70 the issue of the destruction of the Second Temple predominated and could not be avoided. No religious discourse, indeed, no religious life, would then have been possible without attention to the meaning of that awesome event. The message of the apocalyptics was that the all-powerful God who had punished the people for their sins very soon would bring them consolation, punish their enemies, rebuild the Temple, and bring on the messianic age. People who heard this message fixed their gaze upon the future and eagerly awaited the messianic denouement. When confronted by the messianic claim of Bar Kokhba, they responded vigorously, undertaking a catastrophic and hopeless holy war. The rabbis after 70 had a different message. It was not different from that of the apocalyptics in stress upon the righteousness of God, who had punished the sin of Israel. But the conclusion drawn from that fact was not to focus attention on the future and on what would soon come to compensate for the catastrophe. The rabbis sought to devise a program for the survival and reconstruction of the saving remnant. The message was that just as God was faithful to punish sin, so he may be relied upon to respond to Israel's regeneration. The task of the hour therefore is to study Torah, carry out the commandments, and do deeds of loving-kindness. Therefore, from the stubborn consideration of present and immediate difficulties came a healthy and practical plan by which Israel might in truth hold on to what could be salvaged from disaster. Redemption will come. In the meanwhile there are things to do. Just as the Jews awaited a redemptive act of compassion from God, so they must now act compassionately in order to make themselves worthy of it. The tragedy thus produced two responses, the one obsessed with the disaster, the other concerned for what is to happen afterward, here and now.

It seems to me Rubenstein carries forward the apocalyptic, Fackenheim the classical and rabbinical, mode of thinking. The difference between them is not in the contrast between a negative and destructive approach on the one side and an affirmative and constructive one on the other. Rubenstein is not a nihilist, as I have shown. Fackenheim's "commanding Voice of Auschwitz," speaks to people beyond despair, demands commitment from the nihilist himself. The difference is in perspective and focus. In Fackenheim's behalf one must, as I said, point to the remarkable pertinence of his message to the issues of the 1970s. He has, in a way, transcended the tragic events themselves, just as did the first-century rabbis. Fackenheim does not say only the obvious, which is that one must believe *despite* disaster. He holds that the disaster itself is evidence in behalf of belief, a brilliant return to the rabbinic mode of response to catastrophe. In this regard Rubenstein and Fackenheim, representative of the two extreme positions, cannot be reconciled, except within the events of which they speak. Confronting those events, both theologians perceive something "radically" new and without precedent in the history of Judaism. With that shared claim the two extremes come together. What is to be said in response to the claim of both

Rubenstein and Fackenheim that "after Auschwitz" things are "radically" different from before?

First, it must be stressed, other theologians have not been silent. A. J. Heschel, for example, responded to the Holocaust with an immortal Kaddish, *The Earth Is the Lord's*. Milton Steinberg, Mordecai M. Kaplan, and Arthur A. Cohen, among others, take account of the Holocaust without admitting the central contention of the recent "Auschwitz-theologians." They take seriously the problem of evil but regard the problem as posed effectively by any sort of misfortune or by the whole history of the Jewish people, for they find themselves equally disturbed by the suffering of one person as of one million. One indeed may argue that "after Auschwitz" became an effective slogan, along with "never again" and similar allusions to the Holocaust, too long after the liberation of Europe to constitute merely a response to the events of those far-off days and distant places.

But the central allegation is contained in the word "radical," by which is meant that the Holocaust is unprecedented and changes everything. This viewpoint is not shared by Kaplan, Heschel, and others. The most important critique comes in Wyschogrod's review of Fackenheim. There he meets head-on the issue of "radical evil" and, in my opinion, demolishes the constructions of the whole "after Auschwitz" school. Because of the importance of his critique, I quote his exact words at some length:

> I have already termed Fackenheim's enterprise "negative natural theology," a phrase which deserves brief explanation. Traditionally, natural theology has been the enterprise whereby the existence of God is demonstrated on the basis of some rational evidence, without recourse to faith or revelation. Most commonly, the point of departure for such an attempt was some "positive" feature of the world as it appears to man: its order, its beauty, or its harmony. It was then argued that such characteristics could not be the result of pure chance and that it was, therefore, necessary to posit some all-powerful and rational being as the author or creator of a universe possessing the respective positive characteristics ... Fackenheim's point of departure is, of course, the opposite of the "positive." Instead of being the order, beauty, harmony or justice of the universe, it is a totally unique crime, unparalleled in human history. But once we get over this initial difference, similarities appear. In the positive version, a positive characteristic of the

universe is noted and it is argued that no natural explanation for it is adequate. In negative natural theology, an evil pointed out for which also, it is alleged, no natural explanation is possible. Of course, the conclusion in negative natural theology cannot be identical with that of positive natural theology, inasmuch as the problem of theodicy cannot here easily be ignored. Nevertheless, the conclusion which Fackenheim draws, the sacred duty to preserve the Jewish people, is the functional equivalent of the existence of Judaism, a foundation as fully serviceable to the secularist as to the believer. One is almost driven to the conclusion that in the absence of the Holocaust, given Fackenheim's profound understanding of the irreversibility of the secular stance, no justification for the further survival of Judaism could have been found. With the Holocaust, amazing as this may appear, Judaism has gotten a new lease on life.

Wyschogrod, finally, reaffirms the classical position of Judaic theology on the suffering of the Jewish people:

Israel's faith has always centered about the saving acts of God: the election, the Exodus, the Temple and the Messiah. However more prevalent destruction was in the history of Israel, the acts of destruction were enshrined in minor fast days while those of redemption became the joyous proclamations of the Passover and Tabernacles, of Hannukah and Purim. The God of Israel is a redeeming God; this is the only message we are authorized to proclaim, however much it may not seem so to the eyes of non-belief. Should the Holocaust cease to be peripheral to the faith of Israel, should it enter the Holy of Holies and become the dominant voice that Israel hears, it could not but be a demonic voice that it would be hearing. There is no salvation to be extracted from the Holocaust, no faltering Judaism can be revived by it, no new reason for the continuation of the Jewish people can be found in it. If there is hope after the Holocaust, it is because to those who believe, the voices of the Prophets speak more loudly than did Hitler, and because the divine promise sweeps over the crematoria and silences the voice of Auschwitz.

This seems to me all that needs to be said in response both to the "commanding Voice of Auschwitz" and to the joy of "nothingness" alike.

Various unrelated social, cultural, and political phenomena

have been interpreted as a response to the Holocaust. I do not allude to the creation of the State of Israel or to the great "return to religion" of the 1950s—an event much criticized at that time but sorely missed today. I refer to the reaffirmation of Jewish self-interest in times of political crisis, to the recognition that the Jews do have serious interests in political, social, and economic life, and that sometimes these interests come into conflict with those of other groups. I refer to the electrifying popular response to the Six-Day War and the generally favorable reaction to the slogans of the Jewish Defense League, if not to its mindless activities. I refer to the publicity about "freeing Soviet Jewry" and to the obvious sense that in making such efforts people are doing today what they wished they (or someone) had done in the 1930s. I refer to the nonacademic thrust toward "Jewish ethnic studies" in the universities and the students' manifest claim to want to learn something—anything—Jewish. I refer, finally, to the serious efforts of younger Jews to participate, in their own idiom, in the Judaic tradition, to the creation of Jewish newspapers by the university students, to the success of *Response* and similar (if not so excellent) magazines, to the creation of Jewish communes and communities, according to an ideology with (alleged) roots in the ancient *havurot*. These have been exciting events; possibly some may prove important. None could have been predicted a generation ago, let alone in the 1930s. Then it seemed the way ahead lay downward and outward, for the future looked bleak. Today, say what one will in criticism of details of the "ethnic assertion" of young Jews in its several forms, one cannot take a negative view of their devotion to the Judaic tradition and their loyalty to the Jewish people.

But the question is: is the current ferment in Jewish community affairs the result of the Holocaust; is it one of the implications of the Holocaust?

In my opinion, the answer is negative. The "after Auschwitz" syndrome in Jewish theology and the appeal of "never again" in Jewish community affairs both constitute creations of the late 1960s and early 1970s.

From 1945 to about 1965, the Holocaust was subsumed under the "problem of evil." The dominant theological voices of that time did not address themselves to "radical evil" and did not claim that something had happened to change the classical theological perspective of Judaism. The theologians of the day wrote not as if nothing had happened, but as if nothing had happened to impose a new perspective on the whole past of Jewish religious experience. To be sure, the liberal, world-affirming optimism of the old theological left was shaken; Kierkegaard and Niebuhr, through Will Herberg and others, found a sympathetic Jewish audience. But the Holocaust—"Auschwitz"—was part, not the whole, of the problem.

What happened, I think, was the assassination of President Kennedy, the disheartening war in South East Asia, and a renewed questioning of the foundations of religious and social polity. "Auschwitz" became a Jewish codeword for all the things everyone was talking about, a kind of Judaic key word for the common malaise. That—and nothing more. The Jewish theologians who claim that from Holocaust events one must draw conclusions essentially different from those reached after the destruction of the Second Temple or other tragic moments posit that our sorrow is unlike any other, our memories more searing. But they say so in response not to the events of which they speak, but, through those events, to a quite different situation.

And they necessarily select some events, and not others, for the purpose of their theological enterprise. They speak of "Auschwitz," and "radical evil," but not of Jerusalem rebuilt and the dawn of redemption. If the former is a more than merely this-worldly event, why not the latter? But *if* the latter be taken seriously, then why no place for redemption in the response to the former?

Alongside "Auschwitz" comes Fackenheim's emotional claim that "we should not hand Hitler any posthumous victories." The appeal—one can hardly dignify it as an "argument"—is meant to buttress any form of traditional belief or practice that comes to mind. Hitler hated Judaism, therefore we must be religious Jews—an ironic revision of the Talmudic dictum: God is merciful and holy, therefore we must be merciful and holy. "Auschwitz" replaces Sinai.

The argument might enjoy a measure of historical pertinence if Hitler had distinguished among the Jews those who were religious or kept kosher or wore *tzitzit*. But since Nazism ignored the life-style of the Jews and sought only to end all Jewish life, the sole necessary consequence one can draw is that having Jewish babies—however one raises them thereafter—is a defeat for Hitler. The rest is either mere sentimentality or meretricious. It is an argument that cannot be examined, let alone criticized; it is not open to rational inquiry; and it has unlimited consequences. Since Hitler liked Wagner and sauerkraut and did not like to see animals mistreated, are we to give up *The Flying Dutchman* and cabbage and beat our dogs? And if so, why in 1972 and not in 1946?

Classic Jewish theology was not struck dumb by evil and neither changed its apprehension of the divinity nor claimed in its own behalf a renewed demand on the Jews on account of disaster. To be sure, important theological issues require careful, indeed meticulous, attention. But to debate those issues outside of the classic tradition and under the impact of grief can produce few lasting or even interesting results.

In my view, Jewish public discourse has been ill-served by "Auschwitz" without the eternity of Israel, misled by setting the response against Hitler in place of the answer to God who commands, and corrupted by sentimentality, emotionalism, and bathos. These have produced in people less sophisticated, less responsible than either Rubenstein or Fackenheim, vacuous mysticism on the one side and mindless sloganeering on the other. As Elie Wiesel writes in *Legends of Our Time*, "No cocktail party can really be called a success unless Auschwitz, sooner or later, figures in the discussion." In such a setting, "Auschwitz" profanes Auschwitz; the dead are forcibly resurrected to dance in a circus, the survivors made into freaks. It is enough. Let the dead lie in peace and the living honor them in silent reverence. Again Wiesel: "Leave them there where they must forever be . . . : wounds, immeasurable pain at the very depth of our being." Why should they serve the living as a pretext for either belief or unbelief, for a naturalist God or a supernatural God? The truth is there is no meaning in it all, at least none discerned for humanity. The fact is that the living live. The choice is about the future, not the past. Theologians and politicians alike should let the dead rest in peace. We are not well served by the appeal to the Holocaust, either as the rationalization for our Judaism or as the source of slogans for our Jewish activism and self-assertion.

What then are the implications of the Holocaust? In one sense, I claim there is *no* implication—none for Judaic theology, none for Jewish community life—which was not present before 1933.

Judaic theologians ill-serve the faithful when they claim "Auschwitz" marks a turning, as in Rubenstein's case, or a "new beginning," as in Fackenheim's. In fact Judaic piety has all along known how to respond to disaster. For those for whom the classic Judaic symbolic structure remains intact, the wisdom of the classic piety remains sound. For those to whom classical Judaism offers no viable option, the Holocaust changes nothing. One who did not believe in God before knowing about the Holocaust is not going to be persuaded to believe in Him on its account. One who believed in the classical perception of God presented by Judaic theologians is not going to be forced to change that perception on its account. The currently fashionable "Jewish assertion" draws on the Holocaust, to be sure, as a source of evocative slogans, but it is rooted in America and in the 1970s, not in Poland and in the 1940s. It has come about in response to the evolving conditions of American society, not to the disasters of European civilization. Proof of its shallowness and rootlessness derives from its mindless appropriation of the horrors of another time and place as a rationale for "Jewish assertion"—that, and its incapacity to say more, in the end, than, "Woe, woe." "Jewish assertion" based on the Holocaust cannot create a constructive, affirmative, and rational way of being Jewish for more than ten minutes at a time. Jews find in the Holocaust no new definition of Jewish identity because we need none. Nothing has changed. The tradition endures.

6

How the Extermination of European Jewry Became "The Holocaust"

In January 1945, while the gas chambers still were working, people knew that it was all over for the Jews of Europe. Most were dead, the rest dying. Few would survive until spring. At the annual conference of the Yiddish Scientific Institute held that month, the greatest Judaic theologian of this century, Abraham Joshua Heschel, a Jew from Poland, said what there was to be said. What lessons there were to be drawn from the death of European Jewry he did not specify; what lessons there were to be learned from its life he proposed to state.

He asked his hearers how one might appraise the historical significance of the world now ended in smoke and ashes. And he answered: "As Jews, with an old tradition for appraising and judging events and generations, we evaluate history by different criteria, namely, by how much refinement there is in the life of a people, by how much spiritual substance there is in its everyday existence.... We gauge culture by the extent to which a whole people, not only individuals, lives in accordance with the dictates of an eternal doctrine or strives for spiritual integrity; the extent to which inwardness, compassion, justice, and holiness are to be found in the daily of the masses." Speaking of the millions of Eastern European Jews, who had borne the brunt of the massacres, he said: " ... in this period our people attained the highest degree of inwardness ... it was the golden period in the history of the Jewish soul.'' Heschel concluded this oration, which became a book under the significant title *The Earth Is the Lord's* as follows: "Loyal to the presence of the ultimate in the common, we may be able to make it clear that man is more than man, that in doing the finite he may perceive the infinite."

It should not be thought that Heschel addressed the world like a universalist Reform rabbi, speaking "to all humanity, not *only* to the Jews." His was a distinctively Judaic message. The penultimate passage of his oration contained that profound sadness, profoundly understated, which expresses the meaning of a long and often trying history: "Our life is beset with difficulties, yet it is never devoid of meaning.... Our existence is not in vain. There is a Divine earnestness about our life. This is our dignity. To be invested with dignity means to represent something more than oneself. The gravest sin for a Jew is to forget what he represents. We are God's stake in human history.... The time for the kingdom may be far off, but the task is plain; to retain our share in God in spite of peril and contempt."

But there is a Jewish meaning to the massacre of European Jewry which of itself is also a human meaning.

It is that simple affirmation of life in the face of death and that defiance of despair which Heschel expressed, and which he also personally embodied in that cold and terrible January of 1945. For he had been snatched from Warsaw after the Germans had arrived there, and he had lost all of his family. He was the last of them: the witness, the survivor, the brand plucked from the burning, the saving remnant. In his testament is contained the spirituality of Judaism: fully realized, he claimed, in that world which is no more, that world which is only to be mourned. While the dying yet was going on, he entitled his testament, "The Earth Is the Lord's." There is nothing more to say.

How have we come from that defiance of despair, from that affirmation of God's rule on earth and in heaven, to "the Holocaust"? For there surely is a contrast between the dignity and hopefulness of Heschel, who had suffered and lost but endured, and the bathos and obsession of those who, thirty-five years later, want to speak of nothing but transports, gas chambers, a million abandoned teddy bears, and the death of God.

Heschel imputed no enduring guilt to others, whether "the

gentiles," or "the Christians," or "the Germans." Like Leo
Baeck, chief rabbi of German Reform Judaism and another survivor of the concentration camps, he may have wondered
whether the Germans had forgiven themselves. But he knew that
the earth is the Lord's, and affirmed that judgment is God's. A
man who talked of dignity and who understood that we represent
more than ourselves, Heschel spoke with silence. He mourned to
the day of his death. But he loved life, accepted all, regretted
nothing. Having given his testimony, he went on to other things.
The word "Holocaust" scarcely appears in his vast theological
writings. The problem of evil is a problem, but it is no more than
that. Heschel wrote much more on Job than on "Auschwitz."
The stench and human degradation, the unspeakable cruelty and
inexpressible horror—these he knew full well. But he speaks of
dignity and refinement. The epitaph is written not by Hitler, but
by Heschel.

But if Heschel spoke the last word in the closing months of the
war, whence "the Holocaust"? We would look in vain in the
1950s for what some call "Holocaustomania." The Jews were
concerned with other things. There was a return to religion and,
among the second and third generations of American Jews, to the
synagogue. Indeed, Heschel's theological writings of that period
enjoyed a wide and appreciative audience. Describing American
Judaism in the mid-1950s, the great sociologist Nathan Glazer
managed to write an entire book without making more than passing reference to the destruction of European Jewry.

The contrast with the 1970s is striking. Now there is no way to
address the Jewish world without referring to "the Holocaust." It
is taken for granted that that event, bearing meanings all of us
know and none needs to articulate and expatiate upon, exhausts
the agenda for discussions between Jewry and the world at large.

Now, it should not be thought that in the twenty years following 1945 people failed to notice the absence of more than five
million European Jews, who were among more than twenty million European civilians who had perished in the recent war. There
was, after all, the State of Israel, created in part as a refuge for
those survivors of European Jewry who chose to go there and
supported in some measure for its role as a phoenix arisen from
the ashes of the exterminated communities of the Continent. Still
more important, there were many scholarly works and novels,

written both to preserve the events in a factual way and explore their meaning for the life of the imagination. Most important of all, a profound sense of their status as survivors seized world Jewry. American Jews knew that, had their parents or grandparents not left Europe, they too would have been killed. America for them assumed a providential aspect, as did the State of Israel for those Israelis (and they are many) who had lost their families in Poland or Holland or Hungary. So the Jews did not forget. They drew lessons, and taught them. They did not neglect the tasks of mourning and memorialization.

But we do not find in the 1950s what we see today: that obsession with "the Holocaust" which wants to make the tragedy into the principal subject of public discourse with Jews and about Judaism. The refinement, restraint, and dignity of Heschel and his generation have not been taken as models by his successors. There have even been proposals to set up "Holocaust centers" in every Jewish community, complete with buildings, professional staffs, exhibitions, programs, and commemorative events. Such "Holocaust centers" are to function like synagogues. But the faith which brings them into being is not Judaism and its rites, but, rather, one chapter in the history of the Jewish people. One does not have to aim at forgetting the unforgettable in order to judge such "centers" as nihilistic and obsessive, lacking that dignity and faith of which Heschel spoke.

And now we have the President's Holocaust Commission, which raises the whole business above the level of parochialism and provinciality. Just this spring in the rotunda of the Capitol there was a solemn memorial service, a public event within the context of America's civil religion. In so far as America represents itself as a religious nation, with a place for Catholic, Protestant, Jew (and, I hope, Moslem, Buddhist, Russian and Greek Orthodox, and many more), the Judaic component is now defined by "the Holocaust."

Not a few Jews find the Holocaust Commission puzzling. There has not, after all, been a commission created to memorialize the Armenian massacres of World War I (the first major act of genocide in this century), or the political violence and mass murder of Stalinist Russia and Maoist China, let alone the Nazi war against the Poles, Russians, South Slavs, Slovaks, and other people deemed by the racist *Wissenschaft* to be subhuman. And, to be sure, such commissions as these would prove equally puzzling to blacks and Indians on our own shores, who surely would wonder why we commemorate these sorts of acts done abroad, which when they occur in our own land are forgotten.

Since the Armenian people in America shape their distinctive life around their faith and church, and, although mourning for the dead, have yet to found Armenian centers of remembrance of Turkish atrocities alongside their institutions of community and church, we must inquire into this aspect of Jewish activity. What role is "the Holocaust" *as symbol* meant to serve? For it is as evocative symbol, not as historical memory, that "the Holocaust" wins its capital *H* and its quotation marks.

If we want to know what important questions "the Holocaust" answers for American Jews, we have first of all to ask when the sorrow and pain of the European tragedy turned into "the Holocaust." Also we need to discover when "the Holocaust" became a powerful and evocative symbol. When did it begin to bear its own, unexamined, self-evident meanings, to impose its own unanalyzed significance, so that, without reflection, we all know how we are supposed to feel and think and what we are supposed to do? The answer lies in the career of another distinguished theologian of Judaism, Emil Fackenheim. For if Heschel addressed the world which endured the war and personally suffered in it, Fackenheim became the prophet of "the Holocaust" and one of its powerful ideologists. Tracing the turn in his career helps us to isolate the moment of transition from event to symbol.

Before the 1967 war, Fackenheim was known as a religious existentialist and a scholar of Hegel. Fackenheim's books and essays written before 1970 take up established themes of the philosophy of religion and Judaic theology; since that time, however, his work has been dominated by "Auschwitz." To Fackenheim is credited the apothegm, "Let's not hand Hitler any more victories." The practical meaning of that resolution, it is invariably understood, is that Jews should practice Judaism, and Jews and gentiles should support the State of Israel. One of Fackenheim's critics, Michael Wyschogrod, declares that Fackenheim has substituted "the commanding voice of Auschwitz" for the revelation of Sinai, and Hitler for Moses. While this may be somewhat extreme, it contains a measure of truth.

Clearly, something happened to Fackenheim and his audience

between the end of the 1950s and the beginning of the 1970s. This was an experience so fundamental as to impart to the massacre of European Jewry a symbolic meaning, self-evident importance, and mythic quality. Jews had been put to death in unimaginably dreadful circumstances. At the time Heschel had laid stress on dignity and faith in the earth which is the Lord's, by the 1970s, matters had so changed that dignity, refinement, and faith were no longer acceptable themes. The messages had shifted over the years; now the events were made to speak of other things, and to people other than the original victims and survivors.

What turned an historical event into a powerful symbol of contemporary social action and imagination was a searing shared experience. For millions of Jews, the dreadful weeks before the 1967 was gave a new vitality to the historical record of the years of 1933 to 1945—the war and its result. Before June 5, 1967, the State of Israel appeared to be doomed: surrounded, penned within its constricted frontiers by vast and well-armed enemies. Worse still, the State was abandoned by all its friends, whose commitments (made after the 1956 war) to open the Suez Canal and keep open the Gulf of Eilat/Aqaba had proved worthless.

Now, one of the critical points in the "Holocaust" myth (truth told as story) is that European Jews had no place to go. The world abandons the Jews in their time of doom—*and in 1967 it happened again.*

But the story of the extermination of European Jewry could not serve as the foundation for a usable myth of "Holocaust" without one further component. No myth is serviceable if people cannot make it their own and through it explain their own lives; no story of a life can end in gruesome death. A corollary of "Holocaust," therefore, had to be redemption. The extermination of European Jewry could become "the Holocaust" only on June 10, when, in the aftermath of a remarkable victory, the State of Israel celebrated the return of the people of Israel to the ancient wall of the Temple of Jerusalem. On that day the extermination of European Jewry attained the—if not happy, at least viable—ending which served to transform events into a myth, and to endow a symbol with a single, ineluctable meaning.

But this is still only part of the story. For, once "the Holocaust" had taken shape, its suitability for the purpose of the social imagination still had to be fully exposed. It had to explain more then itself; it had to speak to more people, about more things, than it had at the outset. Certainly American Jews and Israeli Jews could not interpret "the Holocaust" in the same way and for the same purpose, without doing violence to the distinctive context in which each group makes its life.

The place of "the Holocaust" in the civil religion of the State of Israel is easy to understand. It forms a critical element in the public explanation of why there must be a State of Israel, why it must be of its present character and not some other, and why every citizen must be prepared to support the State in peacetime and to fight for it in war. The State, then, forms the complement of "the Holocaust," completing and rendering whole that sundered, pained consciousness represented by the humiliation and degradation of the event itself. For Israelis, the myth of "Holocaust and redemption" provides that core of common truth on the foundation of which a society can be built. That it is self-evidently a true myth to Israelis goes without saying.

For American Jews, then, the myth of "Holocaust and redemption" must prove puzzling. They have not drawn the parallel conclusion—that America is that refuge and hope the European Jews should have had—because America was there in the 1930s and '40s, and yet offered no refuge and no hope. They could not declare this country to have contributed a fundamentally new chapter to the history of the Jewish people—at least not in the way in which Israelis declared the foundation of the State of Israel to have inaugurated a new and wholly fresh era. In so far as the myth of "Holocaust and redemption" enters into the self-understanding of American Jewry, it has to answer different questions from those posed by the creation of a state and the sustenance of a society.

I am inclined to see these questions as two separate and distinct ones, the first addressed to the particular world of the Jews, the second to the world at large. But they are not unrelated, for both of them emerge from the special circumstances of the American of Jewish origin whose grandparents or great-grandparents immigrated to this country. For that sort of American Jew, there is no common and acknowledged core of religious experience by which "being Jewish" may be explained and interpreted. Because anti-Semitism as a perceived social experience has become less common than it was from the 1920s through the early 1950s, there is also no common core of social alienation to account for the distinctive character of the group and explain why it continues, and must continue, to endure. Indeed, many American Jews, though they continue to affirm their Jewishness, have no clear notion of how they are Jewish, or what their Jewish heritage demands of them. Judaism is, for this critical part of the American Jewish population, merely a reference point, one fact among many. For ideologists of the Jewish community, the most certain answer to the question of the third generation must be, "There is no real choice." And "the Holocaust" provides that answer: "*Hitler* knew you were Jewish."

The formative experiences of "the Holocaust" are now accessible, also, without learning and without commitment. No person can encounter the events of 1933 to 1945 without entering into them in imagination. It is better to understate the matter. The experience of "the Holocaust" is not something which ended in 1945; it ends when I wake up in the morning, and it is renewed when I go to sleep. And so it is for all of us. These "Judaizing experiences," then, do serve the role Fackenheim has found in them: as Wyschogrod complained, they do take the place of Sinai in nurturing an inner and distinctive consciousness of "being Jewish."

So the first of the two questions before us, the inner one, is the question of who we are, and why we are what we are and not something else. "The Holocaust" is made to answer that question.

The second is a social question: who are we in relationship to everybody else? The utility of "the Holocaust" in this context is not difficult to see, once we realize that the TV counterpart to "Holocaust" is "Roots." It follows that, for American Jews, "the Holocaust" is that ethnic identity which is available to a group of people so far removed from culturally and socially distinctive characteristics as to be otherwise wholly "assimilated." "The Holocaust" is the Jews' special thing: it is what sets them apart from others while giving them a claim upon those others. That is why Jews insist on "the uniqueness of the Holocaust." If on campus have soul food, the Jews will have kosher meals—even if they do not keep the dietary laws under ordinary circumstances.

Unstated in this simple equation, "Roots" = "Holocaust," is the idea that being Jewish is an ethnic, not primarily a religious, category. For nearly a century American Jews have persuaded themselves and their neighbors that they fall into the religious—and therefore acceptable—category of being "different," and not into the ethnic—and therefore crippling and unwanted—category of being "different." Now that they have no Jewish accent, they are willing to be ethnic.

So a profound inner dilemma and a difficult matter of social differentiation and identification work themselves out within the myth of "Holocaust." As to the "redemption" chapter of the story, the State of Israel tells the same truths to American as it does to Israeli Jews. But since American Jews do not, and cannot, infer the same consequences from that story of redemption that Israeli Jews must infer, a certain incongruence has arisen between the two versions. After all, it is difficult to speak much about a redemption which we do not really wish to experience. A salvation which works for others and not for oneself is, in the end, not of much value. Thus the "Holocaust" part of the myth tends to play a larger part in this country than it does in the State of Israel.

With these facts in mind, we can readily understand why, in appealing for the support of Jewish voters, the White House should turn naturally to the formation of a President's Commission on the Holocaust. I should guess that, if the Armenians were sufficiently numerous and vocal to warrant a President's Commission on something of interest to them, it might well take some form other than a commemoration of the tragedy of 1915 (though I do not know what that might be). Clearly, the blacks want something other than a memorialization of centuries of slavery. They want something for themselves, for today—as well they should: a completely equal share, at the very least, in all that America has to offer. For that purpose, a President's Commission, while a pleasant compliment, is worth much less than CETA, the EEOC, or goals for the federal hiring of blacks ("and other minorities").

And so it goes. As Richard L. Rubenstein, a brilliant Judaic theologian of whose thought "the Holocaust" forms the critical center, says in this context, "The most appropriate American memorial to the victims of the Holocaust ought to be a national effort for the understanding of large-scale political injustice and violence." For the issue, properly phrased, of the destruction of European Jewry is the human issue of our unhappy century: how to nurture, in an age of disintegration and destruction, that inwardness, compassion, justice, and holiness in which we perceive whatever is infinite in ourselves.

7

Jubilee in Tübingen

In October, 1977, the Eberhart-Karl University of Tübingen celebrated the semimillennial anniversary of one of the two important events of 1477. The other was not even mentioned.

The anniversary was of the founding of the University of Tübingen. The forgotten event was the expulsion of the Jews from Tübingen. The two are not unrelated. The count of Württemberg in 1477 had made a tradeoff: the citizens of the town of Tübingen—located about twenty miles southwest of Stuttgart, in south Germany—agreed to accept the university. The count agreed to remove the Jews.

It was an odd and curious experience for me to join in the university's jubilee, for, like any Jew, I have a double vision of Germany. Words which for others call up one set of thoughts bring to the surface quite another for me. And then there is the music.

On the day of the *Festakt,* the ceremony of celebration, the medieval streets of the old town of Tübingen filled with several dozen village bands. Most were made up of children. As soon as I saw those quaint costumed bands playing their not-very-quaint Prussian military marches, I found myself transported to the east. I stood on the platform of the Auschwitz railway station and heard the bands playing to welcome the trainloads of victims. Especially to welcome the children.

And why not think of Auschwitz, when, a few minutes before, I had heard a great ceremonial sermon on the theme, *Die Wahrheit macht frei*—truth will make you free. To the words *macht frei* I supplied the Jewish protasis: *Arbeit*. Over the gate of the hell of Auschwitz were the words, *Arbeit macht frei*—work will make you free. To hear first this talk and then that music brought pain beyond bearing.

But what is worth reporting is that the pain was mine alone. I could not express it to my German hosts, not because they would have been offended (that would not have bothered me) but because they would not have heard or understood at all. To them the expulsion of the Jews from Tübingen took place a long time ago; there is nothing worth remembering. The founding of the university that same season—that is something else again. The impact of today's Germany upon the Jew of today is something Germans simply cannot grasp; they have known no Jews. The bad memories of their country's history are not to be mentioned.

Had the students been present, they would have had their say. But the jubilee-celebration was so timed that there would be no students at all. I came toward the end of the vacation, before classes would call back the university's 18,000 young people. Still, more than 1,500 made a celebration of their own, way out of town in a field. Between them and the official, civic celebration stood 1,000 policemen, carrying submachine guns.

But the students set up an exhibition, and in it were pictures of Tübingen in another age. It was not the age of the great Tübingen School—the school which created New Testament scholarship as we now know it, the school which stands behind the massive theological contribution of the Germany of humanism and philosophy. It was the age of Tübingen as the most brown of the brown, the Nazi, universities. Even the students did not present a picture of the Nazi Kittel, who made a fine edition of the Hebrew text of the Hebrew Bible while the Jews were being removed and burned.

In truth, the history that cannot be mentioned means no history can be brought to speech. The ceremonial addresses all focused on current political events—the terrorists, for this was the week of the Lufthansa hijacking—and the overproduction of university graduates, no longer to be absorbed into the economy. There were the high-sounding speeches on truth and freedom, and exceptionally pompous and vacuous hours of greetings by the foreign delegates. (Only three greeted the university in the name of their faculties *and students*—Brown, Colorado, and Wyoming. All the others spoke of faculties or presidents or senates.) No one referred to the brown days of Tübingen, and, therefore, none to the golden days of the Tübingen School of the nineteenth century either. You have the one without the other. So there will be no history at all on the occasion of the university's five hundredth anniversary.

My own lectures, delivered for the Protestant theological faculty, dealt with Judaism in ancient times, in the early centuries before and after the beginning of the Common Era. Tübingen today is the center of that approach to New Testament which draws richly upon the Judaic evidences of the period of the founding of Christianity. Among its scholars, both young and old, are distinguished masters of the study of Hellenistic Judaism and its sources, the Dead Sea Scrolls, and other Jewish writings of the period. These lectures were the theological faculty's contribution to the celebration, part of the official program. There can be no doubt that the prominent inclusion of Judaic studies was meant as a powerful statement of rejection of one past and affirmation of another. Tübingen, after all, also was the home of Adolph Schlatter, one of the earliest New Testament scholars of rabbinic sources. One of his principal monographs dealt with Yohanan ben Zakkai. To be sure, the monograph was only marginally competent; its clearly theological bias was evident. It is not history but a curiosity of history. Still, there was Schlatter, and today there are others with a keen interest in Judaic sources and a desire to hear about them.

But even to those who approach Judaic learning with the best will in the world, Judaism is a dead religion, and Jews are a people of some other place. Germany provides virtually no encounter between a vigorous and self-respecting Judaism, on the one side, and an equally vigorous Christianity, on the other. The stray Israelis who come by do not much change the picture; some of them are perceived, even by the Germans, for whom a Jew can do no wrong, as charlatans. Christianity, for its part, is established, a state-supported religion.

To be sure, it is not one religion. The Reformation is still alive. The Catholics in the *Theologicum,* the building housing the theological faculty, occupy one floor, the Protestants another. Since I was invited by the Protestants, I began to think of myself as one of them. In a celebration of the Catholic faculty of the same jubilee, I looked around the room and remarked to the dean of the Protestant faculty, "You know, you and I are the only Protestants here." At the moment, it did not seem funny. Because the two Christianities have long memories, there is yet another past one cannot mention. In the cathedral of Münster, I am told, cages in which free-church dissenters were suspended in mid-air while they starved to death are still displayed. The display seemed in poor taste to my informant, a free-church dissenter from America.

So many histories we cannot confront! While I was in Germany, the abduction of Schleyer had not yet led to his murder. I remarked rather casually that I would not be heartbroken if that leader of the Hitler youth and member of the S.S. were to die; Germany would have one Nazi less on its hands. Again, in Berlin, at an art museum which, in New York or Boston, would have been filled with young Jewish people, I felt again the pain of holocaust, the utter absence of Jews. And I remarked on it to my host: I see no Jewish faces, except in the pictures (work of the 1920s). And again, in Tübingen, when I did observe that there was, after all, a double celebration, one happy, the other sad, once more I found the same response. In these three, and in other instances, it was an absence of response. Nothing was said, no emotion indicated even in the face, in a gesture. If I had said something one does not say, even that was not communicated in a way in which I might perceive it.

But, of course, I knew I *had,* just as I knew I had to. This became clear when, in Berlin, my host's wife returned from a vacation on the island of Rhodes, and I remarked, when looking at the pictures she brought back, that before World War II, there had been quite an interesting Jewish community there. But the people had all been shipped north, and most died even before reaching the death camps, having frozen to death. This seemed to me something important and memorable, something worth saying when speaking of the island of Rhodes. There was no comment.

Once more in Berlin—where I also gave a lecture—this time for the Free University and the Evangelische Hochschule (Protestant divinity school)—I stood with my host looking east, across the wall, at the other side. He remarked that some of the great cultural institutions are being built near the wall so that, if Germany is reunited, they will serve the East as conveniently as the West. I said, "True, but they will melt, since there can be no reunification of Germany without an atomic war. In any case, it is in the interest neither of the USSR nor the USA, nor indeed of Europe, for such a reunification to take place. After all, from 1870 to 1945 we did have a single Germany, and it did not make for the stabilization of Europe, did it?"

These long, long thoughts of world historical forces and powers did not win the attention of my host. Nor did the apocalyptic scene toward the Brandenburg Gate, a long mall, with parks on both sides, presently used, I was told, mainly by roving prostitutes. That is where the West comes to an end: no history, no human connection, no commitment, no emotion, at the empty spaces on the edges of a beleaguered city, filled in by the denizens of hell.

There really was a holocaust.

Part Three

Response to Freedom II
The Place of Zionism in American Judaism

Introduction

One half of the "myth of Holocaust and redemption" has now been fully spelled out, so we come to the other half, which is symbolized by the use of the word "Israel" to refer principally not to its historical referent, the Jewish people, but rather to the State of Israel, the Jewish state. When we speak of the State of Israel, however, we immediately have to take up the internal theory of the relationship between the State of Israel and the people of Israel, the Jewish people, which is fully spelled out in Zionism. Zionism is the name of that movement and that body of ideas which brought the State of Israel into being and which explained, and continues to work out, why Jews throughout the world have a special relationship and responsibility to the State of Israel. To discuss the place of the State of Israel in American Judaism is to raise the question of the centrality of Zionism in the Judaism which shapes the way of life and world view of American Jews. The reason is very simple. Nearly all American Jews are not only supporters of the State of Israel. They also regard their own "being Jewish" as inextricably bound up with the meaning they impute to the Jewish state. Within that simple fact we find the explanation of why nearly all American Jews are, plain and simple, Zionists.

But that fact complicate matters. For Zionism maintains that Jews who do not live in the Jewish state are in exile. There is no escaping that simple allegation, which must call into question that facile affirmation of Zionism central to American Judaism. Zionism further declares that Jews who do not live in the State of Israel must aspire to migrate to that nation or, at the very least, raise their children as potential emigrants. On that position American Judaism chokes. Zionism moreover holds that all Jews must concede, indeed affirm, the centrality of Jerusalem, and of the State of Israel, in the life of Jews throughout the world. Zionism draws the necessary consequence that Jews who live outside of the State of Israel are in significant ways less "good Jews" than the ones who live there.

Now all of these positions, commonplace in Israeli Zionism and certainly accepted, in benign verbal formulations to be sure, by American Jews, contradict the simple facts of the situation of American Jews and their Judaism. First, they do not think that they are in exile. Their Judaism makes no concession on that point. Second, they do not have the remotest thought of emigrating from America to the State of Israel. That is so even though in ceremonial occasions they may not protest when Israelis declare that to be their duty. Third, they may similarly make a ritual obeisance to the notion of "the centrality of Israel," meaning of the State of Israel. They may do so even understanding that that proposition carries the corollary of the peripherality of the *Golah*, in general, and of the mighty community of American Jews in particular.

Looking at Zionism and its Israeli corollaries we should hardly predict that, at the heart of the hope of American Judaism, lies so egregious, so contradictory, so remote a set of propositions as Zionism lodges there. If, therefore, "the Holocaust" accommodates so poorly as an explanation of the human existence of American Jews, redemption—the salvific myth, hope, and rite—as defined by Zionism fits still less well. There can be no accommodation, nor is it possible to adapt so intractable a vision of Jewish existence as the Zionist one to the commonplace realities of American Jews. So that is the question to be faced: why "the Holocaust" of the past with the faraway salvation of the State of Israel? And, once more, we must ask what we learn about American Judaism and the social and imaginative world of American Jews from the particular mythic framework within which they live out their lives, by which they explain themselves.

To begin with the fundamental issue, I must raise the question of exile. If after all, there is to be a Zionism, it must contain the principle of Zion. And Zion without non-Zion, a Land without an "outside-the-Land," is not possible. One catagory creates the other. For Zion is exclusive and, in the nature of things, also wholly locative. There is no Zion in Heaven. It is here on earth, in the material reality of the Land and State of Israel. So too there cannot be an "exile" solely within, an existential alienation given concrete, material reality by a merely aching heart. Alienation and exile are bedmates. But they are not one flesh. And Zionism speaks of the flesh, the this-worldly political facts of Jewish existence. So at the outset we confront the simple question, Are American Jews ("we") in exile? The real question is what use the notion—the Zionist notion—of exile may have for American Jews. The answer given here is not a Zionist answer. It cannot be one. For the locative category, *Golah,* exile, and the utopian one, *Galut,* being-in-exile, derive from the theology of Judaism and deserve a still-Judaic referent, even in this time and place.

Without the definitive category of exile, the question of the place of Zionism in American Judaism becomes still more compelling. That is why the ninth paper, "A New Heaven and a New Earth," must follow the eighth, "Are We in Exile?", even though, from the viewpoint of the unfolding argument of this book, it should stand at the outset of this group, parallel to "The Implications of 'the Holocaust'" in the previous part. What vision of the world so captures the attention of American Jews as to make the Zionist perception persuasive now requires specification. Here too we have to try to make up or allude to the story— retell the myth—which encapsulates the matter. Once more it is the story of people who do this-worldly things but take onto their shoulders a prophet's cloak, a philosopher's mantel. It is the tale of people who with perfect confidence in their righteousness seek salvation and pursue it. Yet it must be said that that part of the Jews' existence susceptible to the salvation afforded by the vision of "Zion redeemed" and the salvific work of Zionism is not the whole. Zionism promises insufficient redemption. It solves only some problems, not all of the anguish of the human and Jewish condition.

Then some may conclude that Zionism, taken seriously and not merely given ritual assent, is hopelessly in contradiction with the facts of American Jewish existence. Indeed, that may well be so.

But it also is a fact that Zionism is the single most powerful and important movement in the history of the Jewish people in the present century. The creation of the State of Israel is universally acknowledged among Jews to be the single most important achievement of the Jewish people in this time—that and not the human achievement of American Judaism. So there can be no evasion of the Zionist challenge to American Judaism, the Zionist defiance of American Jewry's comfortable and complaisant situation. On the contrary, a Zionist theory of American Jewry, if such can be coaxed out of the intractable, arid soil of Zionist slogans and ideologies, becomes necessary. For without a Zionist understanding of itself, American Jewry cannot draw into a single frame of reference its own sense both of the circumstance of Jewry in this world, and of the situation of itself in this country. But out of structural contradictions what sort of ideology is to come?

The argument of the final paper here, "From Sentimentality to Ideology," is that a Zionist approach to American Jewish existence becomes possible when there is a hierarchy of concerns, a ladder leading upward, with many rungs. No Zionism can ask itself to deny the importance of taking up the life of the Jewish state. None can speak of a central point other than Jerusalem. Any theory which purports to be Zionist and deem Shaker Heights or Glencoe, Beverly Hills or Newton, somehow to stand on that same elevated plane of Jewish and Judaic fulfillment as Rishon LeZion, Petach Tikvah, or Mevessaret Zion ("First to Zion," "Gate of Hope," "Zion's Messenger") hardly deserves to be taken as a serious construction. For there are givens. These, in the present instance, define what would be ludicrous. Zionism as an expression of utopian ethnic loyalty and that alone clearly will not do. Zionism shorn of Zion is not possible. But a wholly locative Zionism, consisting solely of emigration and repeating only slogans about a centrality all concede and none perceives, also is not useful. These are the boundaries of argument: utopian Zionism, an oxymoron, and locative Zionism, a necessity but an obstacle.

8

Are We in Exile?

Galut as an approach to the interpretation of American Judaism is politically irrelevant, socially pernicious, economically dysfunctional, religiously meretricious, but essentially correct. For *Galut* essentially speaks of alienation, disintegration, and inner strife. American Jews politically, socially, and economically stand within the corporate limits of society; they do not see themselves as temporary residents, people who really belong somewhere else. Their homeland is America; its turmoil is theirs; so too its tragedy and triumph. To allege that in the eschaton they will magically be lifted up and transported on eagles' wings to some other place is to present American Jews with a useless fantasy. One might as well tell them stories of Sinbad the sailor and call them theology, or history.

But speak of alienation and one addresses the center of the Jewish situation. American Jews are in *galut,* exiled from the joys and glories of Torah, their spiritual homeland. They have lost the art of dying and the public pleasure of celebration together, the glory of a day of rest together, the splendor of perpetual awareness of the natural cycle, above all, the capacity for atonement and the certainty of forgiveness. They have no shared myth within which to explore life's private mysteries, through which to locate the meaning of public events and of felt history. Their mythic life is insufficient. Their most abysmal exile of all, therefore, is from the human quest for meaning.

The existential dimension of *Galut* thus encompasses the situation of the American Jew as modern man. Having lost the capacity unselfconsciously to participate in tradition, the modern Jews—whether here or in the State of Israel—find themselves lost and virtually helpless. They cannot go backward, but see no way forward. The insights of tradition into the human condition, while sound and perpetually correct, come in symbols to which they cannot respond, garbed as absolutes to which they cannot submit. So they pathetically limp from cause to cause, ideal to ideal, drawn in the currents of searching humanity, from one headline to the next. This is the contemporary counterpart to the wandering of the Jewish people from land to land, the former incapacity of Jewry ever truly to settle down. Political *Galut* is a paradigm for the existential *Galut* of our own time. And both mirror a deeper side to the human heart—the soul's incapacity ever fully to accept, to love, not only the other, but, to begin with, the self. If in former times the collectivity of Israel saw itself as alien to its situation but at home in its religious community, today nearly the whole Jewish people has exchanged political *Galut* for one that is more comfortable and secure, if in a measure also self-pitying and narcissistic: alienation from the art of living.

But these reflections on *Galut* have carried us far from the accepted range of discussion. Let me give blunt answers to the questions on the conventional agenda.

The traditional concept of *Galut,* phrased in either historical-political or metaphysical-Kabbalistic terms, does not and cannot characterize American Jewry. It would be pretentious to elevate the banal affairs of a bored, and boring, ethnic group, unsure of its identity and unclear about its collective purpose and meaning, to a datum of either metaphysical or even merely historical hermeneutics. American Jewry simply does not add up to much. Its inner life is empty, its public life decadent. So to whom shall we ask the ultimate questions of meaning? To what shall we apply the transcendent symbols of exile and alienation? To Bar Mitzvah factories and bowling clubs? It would be not merely incongruous but derisive.

At home in American or Western civilization? Alas, as much at home as anyone. Why abstract ourselves from the generality of man? What choices do we have? In all the world, who aspires to something other than our civilization, our way of living? Shall we repudiate jet planes or penicillin or liberal democracy? For what? The oxcart, the medicine man, and the messianic general? Do these improve the human condition?

And if we were to migrate to the State of Israel, what gain should we hope for? To be a Jew in America is no harder than to be an American in Israel, but, whichever one is, he or she remains in the situation of exile. Only propagandists seriously ask us to interpret *Galut* so crassly that its effects may be washed away by a trip across the oceans. No baptism there, nor a new birth in a new world. The new creation, new heavens, and new earth—these are harder to attain.

It follows that Jews whether at home or in the State of Israel cannot repudiate their millennial history of *Galut* any more than they repudiate their truncated history of "enlandisement." Having, and not having, a land our "own"—both are integral to the Jewish experience of history. The felt history of the Jewish people is single, unitary, integrated: the experience of one people in many places and circumstances, not one of them barren of meaning and insight. They all of them constitute the Jewish testimony on the history of mankind, with most of which the Jews are coextensive. Shall we now be asked to say the lessons of the land are true but the lessons of *Galut* are false? Are not the great monuments of our spiritual and intellectual history both in the land and outside of it? And do we not give up our responsibility to stand outside of and to judge the history and works of mankind, if we repudiate our own creation within that history and among those works? And that creation is in a measure the capacity to live as strangers at home.

Galut has nothing to do with whether or not the Jews are fully accepted "as human beings," for it is not created by the world and cannot be changed by it. But for my part, if I am accepted as a "human being" and not as a Jew, I do not accept that acceptance. I aspire to no place in an undifferentiated humanity and hope never to see the end of significant differences among men. The only "acceptance" worth having is of myself as I am, first, last, always a Jew, son of my people as I am son of my father, and, I hope, progenitor of Jews as well. Take me despite my Jewishness and there is nothing to take. Overlook what is important to me and you obliterate my being. Of that sort of acceptance we have had enough in the liberal sector of American society. It has yielded self-hatred and humiliation, and, for Jewry at large, an inauthentic existence. So acceptance of the Jews "fully as human beings" not only intensifies but also poisons the awareness of *Galut*. It denies to us our dignity, our loyalty, our right to be ourselves.

Nor does anti-Semitism do much good, for exactly the same reasons.

Granted, *Galut* ends "with the living of an authentic Jewish existence," but that life is not to be defined by where it is lived. What matters is how. By "authentic" and "Jewish" one may mean many things. To me an authentic Jewish life is one of joy and gladness, a life that fulfills the many-splendored hopes of humanity with the light of Torah. And Torah illumines the world, no one part more than another. American Jews will have attained an "authentic Jewish life" when they look forward to Sabbaths of contentment and festivals of rejoicing, when they celebrate natural glories and share the human pathos, when they have so educated themselves that whatever happens enters into Torah and also explains its meaning.

The end of our exile—and the exile of Jews wherever they may be—will come with the end of alienation, disintegration, and inner strife. On that distant day we shall be at one with ourselves, at one in society, and at one with God. We will know the joy of Torah in the private life and for the public interest, and Torah shall open the way to God. And the first step on that long, long road is the start of the search for the joys of being Jewish—trivial, humble pleasures, such as welcoming the sunset on the eve of the Seventh Day and singing songs about the Lord, master of the world, rock of whose goodness we have eaten, the honored Day. Song without belief, to be sure, but the song contains all the belief we need. Our voices, our words, our melodies—these resonate as one—the echo of our ultimate unity, the end of our exile from ourselves, the beginning of the inner peace we seek.

9

A New Heaven and a New Earth

> Then I saw a new heaven and a new earth, for the first heaven
> and the first earth had passed away...
> And I saw the holy city, new Jerusalem, coming down out of
> heaven from God, prepared as a bride adorned for her hus-
> band...
> And death shall be no more, neither shall there be mourning nor
> crying nor pain any more, for the former things have passed
> away.
>
> Revelation 21:1–14

The new Jerusalem, promised in Isaiah 65:17–19 and 66:22, and
envisaged by John of Patmos, has proved an evocative image for
twenty centuries. It also helps us to understand the Jewish mind
of our own day, for we live among people who have yearned for,
and then beheld, the new Jerusalem.

I refer, first of all, to the creators of the State of Israel, bril-
liantly described by Amos Elon, in *The Israelis: Founders and
Sons* (N.Y. Holt, Rinehart, and Winston, 1971)—the romantic
messianists who realized their dream and attained their eschaton.
Elon's account of the founders is pertinent to American Jewry,
for the same Jews who created the State of Israel also created the
American Jewish community as we now know it. They were the
emigrants from the heartland of world Jewry, the East European
shtetls in Poland, Lithuania, the old Austro-Hungarian empire,
White Russia, Rumania, and the Ukraine. (In this connection may
I recommend Raphael Mahler, *A History of Modern Jewry,
1780–1815* [N.Y.: Schocken, 1971], an extraordinarily rich account of the various communities of European Jewry, especially
in the east, in the modern formative period.) Those emigrants,
whether to Palestine or to America, endowed their movement
with more than this-worldly, rational meaning. They fled not star-
vation but hell, and their goal was not a better life, but the Prom-

ised Land. Elon's account is high journalism: colorful, evocative, always interesting, frequently artful. But he has supplied us with more than an occasional tract; he has given us a portrait of two generations of exceptional interest. From the perspective of modern Jewish messianism, it is the first—the founders'—that matters.

For the founders were men who lived for a cause. They had little in the way of private lives. Theirs was a public task, a public arena. "Few had hobbies; hardly anyone pursued a sport . . . they pursued and served the idea of Zion Revived. Socialists and Zionists, they were secular rabbis of a new faith of redemption"—so Elon.

One cannot improve on Elon's description of these seekers for the new earth and the new heaven:

> Resolute and resourceful abroad, at home they often fought one another with a ferocity that seems to characterize the infighting of most revolutions. In their lifetime historical processes normally much longer had shortened sensationally.
> They had lived their Utopias in their own lives.

What was this Utopia? It was the Jewish state, no less. What reasonable man in nineteenth-century Poland could take seriously such a notion, such an aspiration? The condition of the country was pitiful. Why bother?

The answer was, Because it is time to bother: "Zionism profoundly affected the lives of men. It gave people, thus far powerless and disenfranchised, a measure of power to decide their own fate." And it gave them something to do—a sense that their private lives might be spent in a great, public, and meaningful cause. It further lent to the otherwise inconsequential affairs of small people a grand, even transcendental, significance. Zionism meant more than messianism; it transformed the worldly and natural to whatever modern, secular man may perceive as the other-worldly and supernatural. That is what makes Zionism one of the more interesting movements in the history of religions in the postarchaic epoch.

What has characterized the postarchaic epoch, if not faith in the twin myths of secularity and democracy? The latter would open society to all peoples, the former would make the open society worthwhile. But, as Elon writes:

The crucial experience which lies at the origin of Israel as a modern state was the persecution generated by the failure of emancipation and democracy in Europe. Its myth of mission was the creation of a new and just society. This new society was to be another Eden, a Utopia never before seen on sea or land. The pioneers looked forward to the creation of a "new man." A national renaissance, they felt, was meaningless without a structural renewal of society.

Zionism therefore represents the *rejection* of modernity, of the confidence of modern man in democracy and—because of Zionism's espousal of a "myth of mission" and a renaissance of society—in secularity. For there is nothing wholly secular about Zionism, and there never was. It is not modern, but the first of the *postmodern* religious movements.

The Zionists, so devoted to that dream, did not take seriously their dependence, in the realization of that dream, on others who spent their lives in "real" world. Seeing only visions, they did not perceive their time to dream was paid for by more practical people, who also wanted a dream, one to be lived by others to be sure, and who were willing to pay for the right to a fantasy. Elon portrays Baron Edmond de Rothschild (1848–1934):

> He resented his colonists' European clothes and wanted them to wear the local Arab dress; he insisted they observe meticulously the Jewish Sabbath, dietary and other laws of orthodox Jewish religion, which he himself . . . ignored.

Rothschild was the model for American Jewry later on: "We shall pay a ransom for the absent soul. In exchange, give us pride, purpose, a trace of color and excitement for unheroic lives. We shall pay you to be the new and courageous Jew—to keep the Sabbath on a dangerous hill, to wear *tefillin* in a tank." Rothschild too was one of the founders; he too lives on. Elon calls the founders "beggars with dreams." But they were honest brokers of dreams. And what they promised they delivered. In time they invested world Jewry with new purpose, gave meaning to its endurance, promised hope in its darkest hour.

These are, as I said, the attainments of a religious movement. Throughout Elon's account one discovers the evidences of a new rite, a new cult, along with the new myth. He stresses, for example, that the changing of names was not mere routine:

The Zionist mania for renaming was too widespread to be dismissed as a mere bagatelle. The new names they chose were too suggestive to be ignored as elements in the complicated jigsaw that represents the transient sensibility of an epoch. Names are elementary symbols of identity. They are seldom the heart of the matter, but they often shed a sharp light on where that heart can be found. . . . A Zionist settler, in changing his name from Rachmilewitz to Onn ("Vigor"), was not only Hebraicizing a foreign sound. He was in fact re-enacting a piece of primitive magic, reminiscent of the initiation rites of certain Australian tribes, in which boys receive new names at puberty and are then considered reborn as men and the reincarnation of ancestors.

Likewise the communities they founded were religious communes:

David Horowitz . . . compared Bittania to a "monastic order without God." It was no simple matter to be accepted as a member; candidates passed a trial period, a kind of novitiate. Horowitz likened Bittania to a "religious sect . . . with its own charismatic leader and set of symbols, and a ritual of confessions in public reminiscent of efforts by religious mystics to exorcise God and Satan at one and the same time."

No wonder, then, that the impact of Zionism is to be measured not merely in this-worldly matters. Zionism did more than create a state, a country, a government. It regenerated a whole people. That the day of Zionism, in the form of which I speak, is past does not mean the movement is dead. It does mean that, for the second and third and later generations, its myth, evocative symbols, cult and rites are to be revised and reworked, so that, as once the faith corresponded to experience, once again experience, the workaday world, may gain a new meaning and a renewed interpretation in terms of some other, pertinent myth. Otherwise, how will people abide in the new heaven and the new earth, finding it so much like the old?

But the Israeli founders are not the only people who yearned for and then beheld the new Jerusalem. The American Jewish "founders" share the vision, if from afar.

I refer to the senior generation of American Jewish leadership, the men and women from about forty-five upward, who give, then allocate, the funds, make the decisions, and guide the destinies of

American Jewry. Why do they give sacrificially? Why do they then divide funds suicidally? Why do they make the decisions that have led American Jewry to its present impasse?

The leaders, the decision makers, would not phrase the question as have I. They think they have neither misled the community nor made decisions leading to the atrophy of American Jewry, but led with an accurate vision and decided upon a favorable future. Above all, they claim, rightly in my view, to have sacrificed by giving time and energy and wealth beyond their means—whatever tax benefits served as an inducement—to Jewish Federations and related causes. Before we ask why they do what they do, let us briefly characterize the people of whom we speak and the things in which they believe.

Before us stands the president of a Federation or a synagogue or a Hadassah chapter. He or she has devoted most of his or her spare time—and much time that could not be spared—to the raising of funds for these and similar good causes for twenty years or more. If a woman, she has given up many afternoons and nights to the business of her organization, has attended conferences of states, of regions, and of "national," has badgered speakers to speak for nothing and merchants to contribute to rummage sales, and all for the good cause. If a man, he has patiently moved through the chairs of the communal structure, on the board of this client agency, president of that one, then onward and upward to lead a "division" of a "campaign," then to head a campaign, to sit on the board. Above all, both men and women have found for their lives transcendent meaning in the raising of funds for Jewish causes.

Mr. President, Madam Chairman—both have exhibited not only selflessness but also iron determination. They have enjoyed the good conscience of those for whom the holy end justifies all legitimate, and some marginally legitimate, secular means. They worked for a salvation of which they were certain, and it was, despite appearances, not of this world. This is what makes them interesting in the history of Judaism, not merely banal or trivial. The decision makers of American Jewry have seen a vision and kept alive its memory. They have dedicated their lives to the realization of their holy vision, just as much as the students of Torah in another place and time gave their lives to the study of Torah—for all, a salvific enterprise, an exercise in the realized eschaton, in heaven on earth. They did not see their lives as trivial, their works as unimportant, because *their* lives were spent on significant things—not for them the beaches of Florida, the gambling tables of Nevada—and their works were for a sacred goal.

Superficially, these claims seem extravagant. What transcendent importance is to be located in the activities of the mattress makers' division of the local Federation? Of what salvific consequence the leisure time activities of a pants manufacturer in Hoboken? What great goals are perceived by men who spend their lives filling holes in teeth, litigating negligence claims, or running a store? How has madam chairman attained the end of days, merely by meeting her quota?

Indeed, one may further ask, what justification *ought* to be required for the good and useful lives of the Jews' decision makers? They have made things happen, good things. They rightly claim to have helped improve the world. The better one knows the decision makers, the more one both likes and admires them. They constitute a benevolent oligarchy, exercising the benign despotism of men of good will.

But they themselves claim to be more than merely good and useful people. They see themselves as engaged in serving a cause of salvific valence, whose righteousness confers upon them enviable certainty, a sense of worth beyond doubt or measure. If one cannot argue with them—and one cannot—if one cannot suggest alternative solutions to present problems or even propose that new problems face Jewry—and one cannot—then in them one confronts the Jewish elect. These saints are as certain of their vision of the world as were the saints of olden days. Enjoying the certainty of a self-validating vision of the world, possessed of the security derived from the right understanding of perceived history, illuminated by an all-encompassing view of Jewish realities, they are the saved. What is different, or merely makes them feel uncomfortable, lies beyond salvation. So I claim that the self-confidence and self-righteousness of the Jewish decision makers constitute valid testimonies to their mind, their imagination, and their mythic perception.

It is not faith, theology, ideology, for none offers reasons for its soundness, or needs to. It is myth, in that it so closely corresponds to, and yet so magically transforms and elevates reality, that people take vision and interpretation for fact. They do not need to *believe* in or affirm the myth, for they *know* it to be true. In that they are confident of the exact correspondence between reality and the story that explains reality, they are the saved, the saints, the witnesses to the end of days.

The American Jewish myth—fostered by and shared with Israelis, to be sure—is not to be argued with or disproved. It will endure as long as it corresponds to reality and evokes immediate recognition and assent. And it will pass when it no longer seems familiar and illuminating, no longer explains what people experience, because it no longer derives from what they *know* to be true.

The American Jewish myth is to be criticized, however, by these same criteria: Does it correspond to reality today? Has it led to valid policies, to a judicious and prudent interpretation of reality?

The generation under forty-five, and, especially, that under thirty, have given ample testimony of the myth's ambiguity and insufficiency.

It is ambiguous because it no longer fully corresponds to felt reality. Perhaps it should, but a generation that has not known the frightful insecurity of American Jewry in the 1930s and '40s does not appreciate the full depth of the salvation that dawned with the 1950s. That does not mean the younger does not share their elders' devotion to the State of Israel. But it does mean that that devotion is going to have to be elicited by other experiences, other human perplexities and needs, than those of the 1940s and '50s. What has changed is that the State of Israel no longer stands at the end of time or represents the attainment of the long-sought goal. And that is a very considerable change indeed. Some of the former things have passed away. But many remain, for, there and here, Jews still die, mourn, cry, feel pain—because they are Jews.

And the American Jewish myth is, and always was, insufficient, for it failed to cope with and make sense of other Jewish realities, experiences not subsumed within its story. Because they are mortal, Jews do die, mourn, feel pain. The myth of collective degradation and collective regeneration does not say much about salvation from death and pain. It does not endow the

private person and his selfish concerns with transcendent consequence, in a way that the classic Judaic myth was capable of
doing.

The myth is insufficient, too, because it fails to supply an
epilogue: What of life *after* the eschaton? And life is continuous,
for children are born and have to be brought up. What is to be said
to the children about their future? Those who raise their children
for eventual immigration to the State of Israel have found the only
answer wholly consistent with the myth. But the many who do
not, but who do anticipate raising up new generations of American Jews, stand outside the framework of the myth. This produces illusion and hypocrisy. The hypocrisy is that merely giving
money and political support is as central, as sacred, as living in
the land from which the former things have passed away. It is not.
The illusion—and it too is not a little bit hypocritical—is that
American Jewry may look to the State and civic religion of Israel
as its "spiritual center." This is so in times of stress, but not in
ordinary days, when, quite properly, the focus of Israeli life and
culture is upon the perceived realities of its streets, its mar-
ketplaces, its schools. The dominant issues of Israeli life, the
politics that pervades its institutions, the private concerns of
profane time—these, quite naturally, do not correspond to those
of American Jewish life. For in profane time the visceral issues
are not of Judaism, but of making a living and getting along with
people, of raising children and pursuing a career, of visiting with
friends and laughing about life's incongruities, of gossip and ag-
gression, of work and of love—the things people do wherever and
whoever they are, when they are left alone by history.

None would deny that the State of Israel is the major educational resource for American Jewry. There both young and old
may perceive a true a vision of what it is to be a Jew in normal
times and in an everyday world, of the Sabbath when everyone
keeps it by not working, of the State when everyone in power
cares about the Jews, of the economy when no business is Jewish,
and none is closed to Jews. The perception of the state of
normality—this is what American Jews may gain in Israel, not to
mention knowledge of the Hebrew language and appreciation for
the holy land, and, above all, love for the Jewish people.

But if American Jews choose to remain both Americans and
Jewish, then they cannot hope to turn a merely educational re-

source into a center for their spiritual nurture, not because the State of Israel is not worthy, but because it is, of necessity, irrelevant.

The American Jewish myth, therefore, produces unwanted effects. It inspired the older generation to devote its best efforts to Jewish causes, but ensured that those causes would be connected chiefly with the State of Israel, to the virtual exclusion of the legitimate cultural and spiritual tasks of American Jewry itself. It has deprived the home community of all transcendent value and importance and, therefore, made support for equivalent, or less important, institutions away from home. One may more readily raise funds for basketballs for Beer Sheva than for scholarly books for the Jewish students of Brooklyn or of Boston. It is easier to find money to endow a professorship in biology at the Hebrew University than to finance one in Jewish studies in a Jewish seminary in America or in an American University. The spiritual resources of American Jewry are drawn upon, but not replenished, while the material requirements of the State of Israel predominate.

These are effects. The cause is uncritical faith, which prevents rational and prudent consideration of realities, reasonable allocation of resources of spiritual concern and devotion, not to mention money. The reason American Jewry has failed to formulate for itself a mature and self-respecting relationship to the State of Israel is its substitution of faith for reason. It avoids asking hard questions about itself in relationship to the State of Israel for fear of calling into doubt the propositions of the old faith. One demonstrates that one is saved by doing what one is told ("the commandments"), and the consensus of the believers has little place for complexities, difficulties, and ambiguities. I do not mean to suggest that the formulation of a mature and self-respecting relationship with the State of Israel is an easy task. Figuring out how wisely to use both material and spiritual resources—including time and energy and intelligence—so that the State of Israel will not suffer, but also so that American Jewry will not continue to atrophy, is not simple. But none will seriously undertake the work if he will be abused for it, branded not a dissenter but a heretic. And in the community of the faithful there can be heresy, but not dissent.

Do American Jews intend to remain who they are and where

they are? If it is the collective decision of American Jewry to dissolve itself, gradually to be sure, and to remove to the State of Israel, then the appropriate consequences of that decision are to be drawn and acted upon. A formidable case can be made in favor of such a decision.

But if American Jewry chooses otherwise, then it must do the things that will make possible some sort of stable community life in America. Chief among them is the formulation of a myth appropriate to the circumstances of the 1970s and beyond—whatever they may be. But within that myth will have to be a story explaining that there is no new heaven, no new earth, for we shall not claim Washington to be our new Jerusalem. Telling a story to account for peoples' enduring death, mourning, tears, and pain is not going to be easy. Perhaps what made the old myth so formidable was the exclusion of a refined supernaturalism, the inclusion of a gross, man-centered triumphalism in its place. Tears and pain do not testify to the great deeds of man or Israel. And it will be difficult to say much important about them in a this-worldly, ethnocentric myth.

Finding someone to listen to the story will be still harder. For who wants to be told the truth that, there or here, unhistorical, this-worldly, commonplace life goes on? Who wants to face the facts of his own triviality, his incapacity to achieve, or even contribute to the achievement of, salvation? Those who went through hell could well see, descending from heaven, the new Jerusalem. They perceived the metaphysical meaning of the history of their times within the miseries of their daily life. They saw close correspondence between the great and the small, between heaven and earth.

I for one greatly hope the younger generation will be deprived of the everyday experience of the transcendent, if that experience has to take the form of holocaust and redemption. Let them struggle for meaning when history supplies no meaning: Let them live in peace.

10

From Sentimentality to Ideology
The Tasks of Zionism
in American Judaism

The bonds between American Jewry and the State of Israel are firm, yet unpredictable. They fluctuate from year to year, from headline to headline, if the strength of the ties may be measured in the concrete facts of United Jewish Appeal contributions or revealed in the ineffable measures of concern and of caring. There is a minimum, a perpetual caring, if not too much. There is a maximum, a caring which stops short only of *aliyah*. Between these parameters the community as a whole tends to fluctuate. In the immensely diverse life of families and individuals, the fluctuation is even greater.

It follows that we may generalize, but only at the price of committing banality. American Jewry cares deeply for the State of Israel. But American Jewry chooses to live in America. That means, on the one side, that our community will not tolerate in its midst positions hostile to the essential existence and security of the Jewish state. It means, more important, that American Jewry concedes that the State of Israel is *the* Jewish state. And, on the other side, we contemplate the spectacle of a sizable group of people who persist in calling themselves Jewish and in seeking to secure their continued and important existence as a Jewish community, while not choosing to live in the Jewish state. The paradox of that conflict of established self-understandings, between wholehearted support for the State of Israel, on the one hand, and equally profound will to be what they are, which is both

Americans and Jews, captures the ideological dilemma of American Jewry. It explains, I think, why there is no ideology of American Jewry, that is, no theory which explains to American Jews who they are, what they are, and why they are where and what they are.

For any such ideology which ignores the celebration of Jewish nationhood ignores the facts of American Jewish distinctiveness. But any such ideology which leads to its logical conclusion in the celebration of Jewish nationhood—that is, which affirms for American Jewry a single nationality, the Israeli one—is equally unserviceable. Given the powerful force of American nationalism, moreover, an American Jewish ideology which might attempt to distinguish the American state, encompassing diverse peoples or nations, from the American nation, or which tried to define an American nationality encompassing diverse "religious" groups, would be somewhat beside the point. When, therefore, we confront the unresolved dilemmas of American Jewry, we understand the uncertain character of American Jews' relationships to the State of Israel. These merely are symptomatic of the incapacity to discover an American Jewish ideology, which makes sense of both ourselves and our world. The consequence is a community based upon sentimentality, not intellect and mature self-understanding.

We shall understand ouselves best, I think, only if we take seriously the power of American nationality and American culture and realize that we Jews, as always, in all our specificity point to more than ourselves. When American Jews come to the State of Israel, they discover not their Jewishness but their Americanness. That means that for American Jews, Jewishness is a mode and a measure of their Americanness. It is what makes them distinctive and different specifically in the context of American nationality and American culture. But it has now become clear in the public press that the same is to be said of other American communities and subgroups. The Polish American of the third generation is proud of John Paul II, but has not the slightest intention of moving back to Cracow. The Italian American of the third generation speaks some broken Italian and follows what happens in the homeland, but in Italy is perceived, and perceives himself or herself, as American. American blacks in

Africa are American. All of us turn out to be strangers at home. These obvious facts mean that what all of us once were—which is, Jews from such and such a place in Europe, the Middle East, or North Africa, or Italians from the South of Italy or from Sicily, blacks from the tribes of Africa's west coast, or Poles from this district or that—differentiates us from one another. But what all of us now are differentiates us from our diverse pasts, even while it does not make us what we do not wish to be, undifferentiated Americans. The new ethnicism of American culture is possible only against a background of sameness. Now that Jews have no foreign accents, they want to learn Yiddish or even experiment with Hebrew as their "secret" or ethnic language. In other words, the ethnic assertion, which, for the Jews, leads some to the Jewish Defense League and others to Lubovitch, expresses nothing so vividly as it does the profound Americanism, the completed assimilation, of the Jews of America.

It follows, therefore, that when we analyze our ties to the State of Israel, we have to make sense of these ties, in some measure, in the context of American society and politics. This is for two reasons.

First, American Jews receive the world through the same media as others, which are television, the public press, and other neutral means of communication. American Jews, although they are "for Israel," are not "for Israel" in a way, for a reason, terribly different from the way and the reason the generality of Americans will be "for Israel." True, they will be "for Israel" to a far higher proportion than the others. But they receive their knowledge of the State of Israel—as distinct from their attitudes *to* the State of Israel—from the common media of communication. That is why, for example, American Jews in general have never fully grasped the Greater Land of Israel Movement, the aspirations of Gush Emunim, the policy of creating Jewish settlements on what the American press calls "the West Bank," and other points on which, over the past decade, Israeli policy has responded to forces and aspirations unfamiliar, and even inaccessible to Americans in general, and American Jews in particular. If we report that in the main American Jews want what is good for the State of Israel but, as far as they know and care at all, are not enthusiastic about the present government's program in

Judea and Samaria, we report a fact which is something quite distinct from what we state. We merely inform that our understanding of this part of the world reaches us through those eyes which wear neutral spectacles. The vision of the press is not shaped by a Jewish perspective. Even when reporters are Jewish, they cannot be expected to allow that fact to intervene in what they see. Nor should any of us know what we should be seeing, when, as is clear, Americans of the Jewish religion (or, if one prefers, Americans of the Jewish ethnic subdivision) grasp a world laid forth through essentially undifferentiated, therefore by definition un-Jewish, angles of vision.

Second, if American Jews receive the world as do other Americans, it also is true that American Jews have no choice. For they, their parents, their grandparents, and on backward, know no other world. What this means is that their sense of, their response to, the State of Israel is shaped by their sense of themselves as Jews—and not contrariwise. They are Jews in the concrete setting of their home towns and cities, and, as I have already implied, the meaning of the fact that they are Jews is important principally in that local context, where they live. They have little sense of forming part of an international people of long and proud past, *except* in so far as they are the branch or remnant of that ancient past in Wichita or Duluth, a neighborhood of New York or a suburb of Cleveland, Toronto, Montreal, or Chicago. For America is not only an intensely nationalistic society. It is also a remarkably diverse and deeply provincial one. Local loyalties and regional traits are preserved not only by distance and historical circumstance but also by choice, by what makes people feel comfortable. Indeed, given the cultural diversity of the Jewish community, given its class divisions, which run very deep, given its severe tensions about matters of religion and self-understanding, politics and public policy, given the diversity of its Jewish experience and commitment, from total to minimal—given all this, we must be amazed that there is any consensus on anything at all. Yet there is, and it is on only one thing, and that is where I began, the agreement that to be an American Jew is to be "for Israel," but not to be so very much "for Israel" that one actually migrates to the State of Israel for good.

Clearly, much is wrong with the vague consensus, the shared sentimentality, which substitutes for a mature ideology of American Jewry. For one thing, sentimentality lacks the power to define and secure consistent policy. For another, since it rests on how one feels, sentimentality does not turn individuals into a community, or private persons into citizens. There is, indeed, no sense whatsoever of citizenship of, or in, an American Jewish community. No one responds to the claim, for example, that we have everyday, annual responsibilities to carry out together, responsibilities which impose their taxes in the form of contributions. The UJA and other fund-collecting agencies succeed by appeals to motives other than responsibility, citizenship, collective tasks, the common good, and the public interest. It is not to criticize the UJA and the Federations to observe that they do not appeal to a public interest but only to shared fears or fantasies. The fact is that a community as regional, as diverse, as divided as our own has no choice but to reach out to the lowest common denominator—that is, a generalized sentiment that we are "for Israel"—in an appeal to "history-and-peoplehood" lacking all philosophical clarity.

If that is the case, then if we hope to reform and rebuild a community worthy of the name, we have to take that lowest common denominator and build on that. Clearly, to formulate a Zionist theory of American Jewry, one will construct on the basis of what must, at its foundations, be declared a profoundly Zionist attitude, if not of mind, at least of heart and soul. If, as at Babel, for mortar all we have is mud, then that is what we shall use for mortar. It is enough. And the bricks are abundant: the people is there.

Defining the relationship between American Jewry and Israeli Jewry and the State of Israel lies at the beginning of the way toward a mature self-understanding in American Jewry itself. Surely this fact, that the most powerful Judaizing experience in American Jewry of our day remains the existence of the Jewish state, conforms to the historical requirements of the age. That is why I take the occasion of this dialogue (Fifteenth Annual American Jewish Congress Israel Dialogue, Jerusalem, 9 July 1979) to reflect upon not what is wrong, but what is right and true in the shared and reciprocal respect of the two greatest Jewish communities of our day, yours and ours. That explains why it is necessary specifically in Jerusalem to speak of New York, Los Angeles, Philadelphia, Winnipeg, and Boston.

When we turn to Zionist theory prior to 1948 for guidance in how to think about ourselves, we find rich insight. The Zionist critique of the *Golah* and of the situation of *Galut* for Poland or Germany contains much truth for Florida and Minnesota. Indeed, in so far as the great theorists speak truth about the Jewish condition and the Jewish situation, what they say retains enduring relevance. What they teach us, specifically, is simple, basic things. "We are a people, one people." That affirmation places limits on the theory we may formulate of what we are, where we are, and why we wish to be. Western Jews live as "slaves in freedom." Critics of American Jewry, those who perceive its self-hatred and its profound ambiguities about itself, have done no more than to repeat that simple observation. The inspiring record of German Zionism—"wear it with pride, the gold Star"—which shows the power of Zionist theory to secure for Jews self-respect denied by society and removed by politics, suggests something beyond itself. It is how the Zionist idea, exposed, fully articulated, applied, and exemplified, may yet bring life to the confused Jews of the American *Golah*. Finally, the very existence of a solid and extensive corpus of ideas, of Zionist ideas, stands as a testimony against the antiintellectualism, the banal pragmatism, the out-and-out babbitry, of American Jewry and its leadership. When you realize that Zionism is the creation of intellectuals—lawyers, journalists, professors, doctors, and others who make their living by selling what they know—shaping Zionist theory defies reality as we know it. For such slight self-understanding as American Jewry has attained is not the contribution of the intellectuals but of people of affairs, businessfolk, and bureaucrats. These people have led us into the state in which we now are. That is why we appeal to sentiments instead of to ideas; we rely upon unsteady emotions instead of upon ideology.

Zionist theory carries within itself insights of authentic Judaism. To take one concrete example, on rereading Ben Halpern's *The American Jew: A Zionist Analysis,* I am struck by his stress on the conception of *Galut* as critical to the American Jewish ideology. Halpern offers the insight that until American Jews perceive themselves as strangers at home, they will be out of touch with the fundamental self-conception of the Jewish people through its history. The existential dimensions of *Galut,* as a definition of the human condition, are not to be explored so long as the political and social realities of the American Jews as a *Golah*, of American Judaism as in *Galut*, are not acknowledged. Indeed, if American Jews lose the sense that they form a *Golah*, that they are in *Galut*, however they choose to interpret the meaning of these two facts, they lose all possibility of understanding the deepest historical facts of Judaism. There is no reason to despair. For good or ill, the social and political realities of American life make certain that American Jews will not lose the opportunity to preserve their sense of being in *Galut* and of forming a *Golah*. They will not lose that opportunity if they have the benefit of the Zionist critique of their condition and of their context.

I offer Halpern's conception as only one example of how Zionist theory may help us to understand what we are and who we are—and what we may become. It is meant to instantiate my claim that what we need from thoughtful Israelis, those who care about the bond between us to begin with, is the formation of an agendum for thought and inquiry. We need an intellectual program based upon Zionist theory for the past and for the present. It would be difficult to compose a brief program of inquiry, for the issues are many, the intellectual potentialities profound.

Let me point to two parts of the work.

First, a principal task of Zionist philosophy must be to clarify, to unpack the meaning of, powerful and correct slogans of the day. For example, while American Zionism may happily concede the principle of the "centrality of Jerusalem," precisely what is conceded is puzzling. Since, we all know, this affirmation does not extend to the Israeli government's making decisions about the character and conduct of Jewish life in America, we generally assume that it refers to something more "spiritual." But we are not sure what. For their part, a fair number of Israeli scholars assume that when Isaiah speaks of Torah's going forth from Zion and the word of the Lord from Jerusalem, he is talking about the faculty of one or another of the Israeli universities. In point of fact achievement in Jewish scholarship is widely diffused. No one outside of Jerusalem is able to concede the centrality of Jerusalem in each and every discipline of Jewish studies. In some fields excellent work is done. In others what comes forth is naive and arid, a mere academicism. The prestige attaching to things Israeli does not extend to Jewish ideas. In all the Jewish world, who reads a book of theology written in Jerusalem? And what important book of Jewish philosophy has appeared there in a decade? And where in Jerusalem shall we go for powerful ideas for shaping the intellect and soul of the Jewish people? In the perception of significant intellectual figures in the American Jewish community—professors who teach hundreds of students a year, writers who are read, rabbis who are heard, journalists who write for thousands every week—intellectual life in the State of Israel has little to say to American Jewry. If there is a center, surely the periphery must acknowledge it.

This matter of the intellectual limitations of the center leads to a much more painful issue, which is second and last in the ideological agendum.

In all that has been said, one thing has not been mentioned, and that is, *aliyah*. The reason is obvious. When we speak of American Jewry as a *fact* of Jewish history, we do not speak of its proposed dissolution. Perhaps we should. Maybe Zionism has only one thing to say to the *Golah,* which is, to come home. But if we concede that that is the whole and only message of Zionism to American Jewry, we then offer nothing by which that community can explain what it sees in itself, an enduring and important group. I do not, and would not, ask Zionist theory to accommodate itself to the aspiration of American Jewry to persist in a form very much like what it now is. That seems to me to constitute a non-Zionist theory of American Jewry. I reject it. Zionism without *aliyah* is not Zionism. But Zionism with only *aliyah* is not relevant. I reject it because it contains no seeds of reform, no grounds for criticism. I reject it because it abandons the historical, messianic aspirations of the Jewish people. I reject it because such an ideology, promising a merely favorable view of the State of Israel while positing an American Jewry essentially unchanged and unaffected by the existence of the State of Israel, violates the essential reality of the world which is to be explained.

Nor is it possible to speak of Zionism without affirming *aliyah* as the highest expression of the Zionist commitment. Just as Zionism is a measure of the complete devotion of the Jew to being Jewish—so Jewish that, whatever the world proposes, that Jew requires a Jewish state in this world—so Zionism can conceive of itself only through the fulfillment and completion represented by *aliyah*. But there are facts to be dealt with—facts with which we started. One fact is that American Jews in our time have not taken to heart the challenge of *aliyah*. That is a measure of their Jewishness, a measure by which they may be found wanting. A second fact is that American Jews take very seriously indeed the existence of themselves as a distinctive community and the continued existence of the State of Israel as well.

So if we speak of Zionism which is fulfilled and completed in *aliyah*, we cannot pretend to exhaust the agendum of what there is to be said in Zionism, about the Jews. Zionism has much more to say about the Jewish world. And, if truth be told, when Zionism speaks principally or only about *aliyah*, it gains no hearing, merely ritual assent. When Zionist bodies affirm the centrality of Jerusalem and the definition of true Zionism as solely or mainly *aliyah*, sympathetic and friendly American Jews of course share that affirmation. Then they go home. So *aliyah* has become, in the main, an empty slogan, affirmation of *aliyah* an empty ritual, in American Zionism. We must ask whether there are not other, lesser things for Zionism to discuss. I am inclined to think Zionism has much more to tell American Jewry.

That other, longer Zionist account of ourselves has yet to be worked out. The reason is that, when Zionism is equated solely with *aliyah*, then Zionism no longer finds a serious hearing for itself in American Jewry. That is a tragedy for American Jewry, but no gain for the State of Israel either. When in the 1950s Israelis told world Zionism that the only Zionists live in the State of Israel, they did not generate a mass migration. But they did injure and weaken the Zionist movement in the *Golah*. They deprived the Jewish world of the force and power of Zionist theory of Jewish peoplehood, of Zionist understanding of Jewish existence, of the Zionist definition of a hope for the Jewish future.

In many ways we may compare what I believe to be a considerable mistake in Zionist theory to a similar, but now apparently corrected, mistake in Orthodox Judaism. When reform began to take shape, and the Reform movement came into being, Orthodoxy responded out of fear and weakness. Without confidence in its own future, Orthodoxy, with noteworthy exceptions, declared that any change was unacceptable: "The new is prohibited by the Torah." Consequently, whoever did not do everything was declared to be nothing. Now there is a new spirit in the Orthodoxy of the *Golah*, a spirit not of compromise of Orthodoxy but of love of Israel, the Jewish people. The message of Orthodoxy is that there is a scale, a ladder to be climbed. Something is better than nothing. Perfection is not the sole measure of value.

Today, Zionism takes a position as extreme and uncompromising as that of late-eighteenth-century and nineteenth-century Orthodoxy. I am inclined to think that greater confidence in the power of its Jewish message will in time generate a more nuanced, a more diverse, and, in all, a wiser approach to Zionist theory and definition. For if all Zionism is is *aliyah,* then Zionism has nothing to say to those who do not immigrate and can only condemn those who emigrate. But the Jews are not creatures of theory. We are stubborn, and, by any measure, we are mortal and ordinary. A theory for flesh and blood has to take account of the frailties of heart and soul of those to whom the theory is committed, whose existence is explained.

A Zionism consisting not of *aliyah* at the apex but of only *aliyah* turns a harsh and angry face to the great majority of the Jewish people. It is not a Zionism of hope and confidence, of trust and good will. It is not a Zionism which the *Golah* needs. It is a Zionism to be not defied but merely ignored and disregarded. That other renascent Zionism must be a Zionism which addresses itself to the realities of the Jewish world and the frailties of the Jewish people. It must be a Zionism which calls upon the Jewish people to defy reality and overcome frailty. And that renewed Zionism, in my judgment, can lay the foundations for an American Jewish ideology capable of explaining, and sustaining, permanent and mature ties between the largest Jewish community of the world today, on the one side, and the State of Israel, on the other.

Part Four

Toward a Theory of Zionism for American Judaism

Introduction

Now that we have described the situation as one in which Zionism forms a principal part of the Judaism of American Jews, we pursue the matter as an exercise in Zionist theory. For a description of how things look from a distance need not conclude the matter. There is place, also, for illustrating how things are on the inside. This I do by taking up issues confronted by people within the symbolic and mythic world under discussion. That is what I propose now: to enter into the concrete discussion of issues of Zionist theory. I do so even though, at the end, I declare the exercise a failure. For reasons I shall amply both spell out and then (alas) illustrate, I find it is not possible to do the job that needs to be done, to frame a Zionist theory congruent to the fundamental social facts and philosophical givens of American Jews' situation. To state the conclusion at the outset: there can be no Zionism without Zion, and America is not Zion. There can be, and is, pro-Israelism. That is something different. It is much less than is alleged by American Judaism to lie at the center of redemption. To be pro-Israel is to favor redemption. It is not to be redeemed. But American Judaism is a salvific world view and way of life, a redemptive myth and ritual. So it functions for American Jews, so it is: salvation and redemption, not merely an expression of natural good will.

So far I have stayed close to the frontier between description and ideology, sometimes straddling it, to be sure, sometimes not.

In this section I try to move deep into the territory of theory and even advocacy. For the program now is to offer some of those ideas which will make possible a Zionism both true to itself and relevant to American Judaism. The importance of the work already has been fully exposed. The discussion of the place in American Judaism of "the Holocaust" and that redemption constituted by the formation of the Jewish state now is complete. An entire, large community of Jews—the largest, and humanly most accomplished and powerful in the world today—stands committed to the sustenance of the Jewish state. This it perceives not only as a political refuge for those who need it, but also as a source of enduring meaning for Jews throughout the world. That commitment, it now is clear, is not only rich in ambiguity and—let the truth be said—the potentiality for hypocrisy and self-deceit. It also is profound in its power to move people and to shape their program for themselves as Jews. And it is a source for the definition, too, of the character and content of the American version of Judaism. So, in all, the ideological work is not of negligible consequence.

Alas, it also is not easily done. The three papers of this part may not be deemed weak in themselves. But they in no way prove sufficiently strong to bear the ideological burdens placed on them by what has already been said. The opening paper is the one constructive exercise. It takes political Zionism and turns it into something which, in the end, can flourish even without a Jewish state, and surely outside it. To turn the nationalism represented by Zionism into an ethnic assertion, to speak of "the Jewish people" as a homeland, is to evade the facticity of the Jewish state. It is a typical sleight of hand: to ignore the State of Israel and to traduce the simple assertions of all of Zionism, in all its forms, throughout its history. And yet—and yet what is the alternative? It is to *speak* of a Zionism which one cannot *do*. It is to construct a system by definition existentially remote from the locus of one's existence. Since Zionism is far more than a set of formulas and a scheme of evocative rhetoric, the issues are not readily resolved within the iron frame of social reality in contradiction to imaginative perception.

One surely may affirm the peoplehood of Israel, the Jewish people, without the territory of Zionism, outside the realm of politics altogether. One may deem the Jews to be "a people, one people," and ignore the Land, the one and only Land of Judaism and of Israel, the people, for all its history. But this is not what people maintain, and therein is the pain. American Jews affirm it all: the Land, the nation, the tingle down the spine and tears when they hear the song and see the flag. But they have another nearer land, another nation, the one they support and defend, and they sing its songs and with everyone else they know salute (or, alas, sometimes burn) its flag. Once more the bone of emigration sticks in the craw. Again the matter of exile makes for choking. All that is to be said in favor of the first paper here, "A Zionism of Jewish Peoplehood," is that it states the issues honestly and, I hope, starkly: the matter of equal authenticity, there or here, equal legitimacy as Jews everywhere. Zionism may be locative or utopian, not both.

The next two papers prove far less flawed, because they attempt a diminished theoretical program. Indeed, their purpose is analytical, their mode of advocacy, the criticism of ideas. "The Spiritual Center? The Uses of the Circle-Metaphor," takes up the rejected alternative of viewing the State of Israel as the "spiritual center." The reasons for the rejection of this, in my view useless, metaphor are amply stated. The basic objection is not the wrongness of the metaphor but its altogether too broad relevance. For, in truth, everyone everywhere is always in the center of the world—as he or she perceives the world. It is natural for Israelis to see themselves in the center of the Jewish world: it takes little for them to conclude they form the spiritual center. It is equally natural for American Jews to see the world from the American perspective. Any other would be not merely unnatural but distorting. So a metaphor of perception and vision proves useless. Instead of evoking a sense of its own self-evidence, justness, and rightness, it provokes awareness of dislocation. The locative metaphor denied, we try for a utopian one, a metaphor of time, which is universal. The locative metaphor is vertiginous for all but the center.

"Israel and Yavneh: The Perspective of Time" explores a temporal and, so, utopian metaphor. Here I introduce the notion of "Israelism," as distinct from Zionism, to refer to the nationalism of the State of Israel, including (I hope) its non-Jewish citizens, as distinct from the nationalism of the people of Israel, including its vast non-Israeli majority. One more time the issue of the concreteness of the Land and State comes to the fore, as ever it must. But the issue of interpreting the place and significance of the Land and State may be reframed, as I try to reframe it. We have to ask what the times mean, in which such places flourish, what such places mean to the people who live in such a time and who shape them and sustain them and are sustained in them (for Israelis) and by them (for us). Clearly, this cannot be the end of the matter. But I am inclined to think it is to take it a few paces beyond that notion of Zionism as the nationalism of the Jewish people with which we start this, in the end unsuccessful, exercise.

The one enduring result of this deeply flawed discussion is an unintended one. It is to show the inexorable relationship between the prevailing self-understanding of American Judaism and the stubborn status of onlookers and spectators sustained by American Jews. You cannot think of yourself as these people do and also live out to the limits of your self-understanding. Salvation is somewhere else, because it is needed by someone else, by the remnants of "the Holocaust." In the ultimate and radical version currently emerging, these saved remnants then are made into the saving remnant of Israel, people and, I guess, Land too. Then, in such a frame of meaning, what is there to do? American Judaism makes no place for its humanity, except as spectators. But why, then, should people deem self-evident so merely factitious a tale as that of "Holocaust and redemption" told by American Judaism to American Jews? There is a fundamental contradiction between the status of self-evidence and the context of the people who bestow that status upon a particular tale of death and resurrection (rather than upon some other tale). I do not claim to know what we learn about this sector of humanity, let alone about everybody else, from the demonstrated capacity to sustain a world view and (consequent) way of life which are essentially beside the point of the world to be explained and of the way of life to be worked out.

Yet the argument must not be allowed to conclude with a point of merely universal interest. For the concrete, ordinary life and self-understanding of a sizable group is at issue. They place "Israel," meaning the State of Israel, at the center of their self-understanding. And from the State of Israel they hear this is no

Zionism. For there can be no Zionism without Zion. The simple, inexorable logic of that statement cannot be avoided.

But if American Judaism is to be other than a Zionist Judaism, what are its choices? The generative symbols, the myth capable of explaining to people who they are and what they must do—these may once more be focused upon Torah, personal piety, collective sanctity, and the synagogue. But if they are, will they enjoy that pure self-evidence which makes "Israel" credible, indeed compelling as a mode of redemption? For what Judaism in its classical expression demands, which Zionism in its American formulation does not, is personal participation. So we return to that point at which we began.

To be sure, for Israelis the present impasse is no less painful. If Zionism means Zion and that alone, then should their state not be called "the State of Zion"? For *Israel* in the entire history of Judaism has referred to the Jewish people, and the liturgy, from the Psalms to the most current liturgical poetry, understands by "Israel" the entire Jewish people. If Israelis then wish to maintain that they and they alone are not merely Zion, which all must concede, but also the only "Israel," which none can concede, it is a parlous position.

And, further, if Zionism means principally migration to Zion and a life there, then what in the end will join world Jewry to the State of Israel? For without Zionism as the bridge and the binding, what is left? The nationalism of the State of Israel necessarily conflicts with the nationalism of Jewish Americans or Jewish Canadians or Jewish Mexicans, in so far as these kinds of Americans, Canadians, or Mexicans deem themselves to be integral to their homelands, loyal to their states, and bearers of the culture of thier lands. The universal, transnational ideal of Zionism was never meant to create such conflicts for those Jews—and today they are many—who are not strangers where they are at home, not in their own eyes, not in the eyes of their neighbors.

It would then appear that Zionism properly interpreted constitutes nothing other than the reverse of that coin, the obverse of which is incised with the slogans of Canaanism. That is the view that the State of Israel bears no ties to world Jewry at all but only to its own region. So the ideological anguish spelled out in the introduction in this part, and sedulously rejected in the papers which follow, is a pain shared by Israeli Jews and American Jews.

And *Jew* is no more redundant placed after *Israeli* than after *American*. So in the end it is as much in the interest of thinkers of Israeli Judaism as it is in that of the philosophers of American Judaism to reckon with a transnational Zionism—a contradiction in terms, a transcendental oxymoron.

11

A Zionism of Jewish Peoplehood

The Jewish people is my homeland. Wherever Jews live, there I am at home. And Zionism is the highest expression of the Jewish people's will to endure. I am a Zionist because I am a Jew. Zionism is integral to Judaism as I understand it.

These words are not unfamiliar. In one way or another we say and act on them every day. But their meaning and implications have to be searched out. That is my purpose here.

The Jewish people is my homeland. This is neither a social datum nor a political assertion. It is an affirmation of Jewish peoplehood. We Jews form a unique entity, neither wholly a nation, though part of us constitute a nation, nor wholly a religion, though part of us share a common faith, and all of us derive from that faith. We are a group without a common language, and with little that binds us as a common culture. What makes us a group today? It is our international character and concern; we are men and women who care deeply what happens to Jews throughout the world. It is our historical heritage; we are men and women who together come from somewhere. It is our destiny; we are men and women who share a common fate. And it is our hope; we are men and women who believe in making a better world. But it is not these alone, for they are impersonal and too intellectual. We are made a group by something less tangible, less worldly: by our fathers and mothers and theirs, backward in time, who constituted a unique people on earth and who brought us into the world to carry on the existence of that people.

Zionism is the highest expression of the Jewish people. By Zionism I mean the Jewish affirmation, the assertion that Jews constitute one people and that they wish to preserve that people and enhance its spiritual life. In so stating, I repeat the words of Mordecai M. Kaplan (*A New Zionism* [N.Y., 1955: Theodor Herzl Foundation, 1955]): "Zionism has been defined as 'that movement in Jewish life which seeks to foster a capacity among Jews for the living of a more abundant Jewish life.'" Zionism is the means by which the Jewish people have sought "to survive and to remain true to its destiny . . . Zionism is contemporary Judaism in action." Therefore, Kaplan says, "Zionism should treat the establishment of the State of Israel only as the first indispensable step in the salvaging of the Jewish people and the regeneration of its spirit."

From this definition of Zionism, it follows that *we are Zionists because we are Jews.* Zionism is integral to our understanding of Judaism. While Mordecai Kaplan rightly called his exposition *A New Zionism,* it goes back to the third plank in the Basel platform of 1897: "To strengthen Jewish sentiment and national self-consciousness." This is the only unrealized plank; the others—"to promote the settlement in Palestine of Jewish workers, to centralize the Jewish people by means of general institutions conformable to the laws of the land, and to obtain the sanctions of government necessary for carrying out the objects of Zionism"—these have all been realized in the creation of the State of Israel, the Jewish Agency, the World Zionist Congress, and the like. But who would say that hopes to strengthen "Jewish sentiment and national self-consciousness" have reached the same high degree of fulfillment as the others? The contrary is the case, as everyone knows. So the Zionist task of the hour is to carry out that third principle of Basel. Accordingly, "Zionism will be judged by its efforts for Jewish survival more than by its efforts in behalf of [the State of] Israel. . . . No less than our obligation to see Israel through its difficult period is our obligation to defeat indifference, arrest assimilation, combat disintegration, for these dangers are more imminent today than in any previous period in our history." So stated Nahum Goldmann at the first American Zionist Assembly (December 5, 1953).

Finally, let us define what we mean by saying *Zionism is integral to Judaism*. I understand by Judaism "the non-creedal religious civilization, centered in loyalty to the body of the Jewish people, of Zionism.... All Jewish group activities should be conducted in conscious dedication to the solidarity of the Jewish people and the growth of its ethical and spiritual consciousness"—as proposed by Mordecai Kaplan. That definition of Judaism completes the four principles presented at the outset: the Jewish people is my homeland, Zionism is the highest expression of the Jewish people's will to endure, I am a Zionist because I am a Jew, and Zionism is integral to Judaism.

What is surprising is that these simple propositions, stated by Mordecai Kaplan nearly twenty years ago, both accurately conform to the realities of world Jewry today and stand in exact opposition to the regnant views in Israeli Zionist leadership of Zionism and Judaism. It is a strange paradox that what seems here to be mere common sense should appear elsewhere to be virtually heretical. Yet there is another definition of the Jewish people, of Zionism, and of Judaism, and it is one as commonsensical in the State of Israel as Kaplan's is in American Judaism. It goes something like this: the Jews constitute a nation, and that nation is the State of Israel. Therefore to be a Zionist is to participate in Israeli nationality and nationalism, to live in the State of Israel. As to Judaism, it is a religion, and stands apart from Zionism. Judaism as a religion served a good purpose in preserving the Jews in the *Golah;* its remnants persist in Israeli society, to be sure, but no one not "religious" in the Israeli sense is expected to take Judaism seriously. Who has not been told by young Israelis, "We are not Jews! We are Israelis"?

The Israeli conception of Zionism, centered as it is on the support of the Jewish state and that alone, reaches its logical conclusion in the demand for *aliyah* as the central *mitzvah* of Zionism. Everyone recalls Hadassah's dignified protest against the imposition of the requirement of *aliyah* on world Zionism, the effort to define Zionism as a self-liquidating movement, whose leaders are to be only those who are in the last stages of preparation for migration to the State of Israel. We need hardly affirm that *aliyah* is one important component of Zionist activity. Not only so, but it is going to remain high on the agenda of world Jewry. The reason is not only that the State of Israel needs Jews, but also that the

Jews throughout the world have many affirmative reasons for attaching their personal destinies to that of the State of Israel. The issue before us, first, is whether or not to affirm the *Golah* as an integral part of the Jewish world, as an equal partner, with the State of Israel, in the Zionist enterprise. But the larger issue, given our definition of Zionism, is, second, whether we American Zionists have a portion and a place in the land of Israel, and whether we have a part in Judaism. Remember, we held that Zionism is integral to Judaism. If then we can not be Zionists, how can we regard ourselves as good Jews? So the definition of Zionism solely in terms of *aliyah* is not a negligible quibble about words. It is not a political gambit. It is an assertion of fundamental importance and wide-ranging implications. It is nothing other than the assertion that the *Golah* has no part in the Jewish future, in the Jerusalem of the future.

Concentrating on *aliyah* is unfortunate, for many people will find their own reasons not to settle in the State of Israel, just as some will find reasons to do so. But the practical problems of *aliyah* are not to be ignored. Ruth Seligman ("The American *Oleh* and the Israeli Society," *The Reconstructionist*, April 21, 1972) writes, "Many Americans, whether motivated by idealism or pushed by dissatisfaction with their current life, arrive unprepared for the realities of life in Israel. . . . It is understandable why official bodies try to present Israel only in positive terms. There is fear that someone may not come if he knows that the cost of housing is currently exorbitant, that his children may be unhappy their first year in school, or that his wife may both resent the extra hours she needs to devote to the house and also miss the organized and structured social life she had in the States."

The problem of religion cannot be ignored. Since American and Canadian Jews in large numbers are Reform and Conservative, and since they cannot practice Reform and Conservative Judaism in Israel with the support and recognition that Orthodoxy receives, the demand for *aliyah* introduces a certain paradox.

And, too, the new immigrant, in Miss Seligman's words, "is irritated . . . by the rudeness of the drivers, the aggressiveness of the people, the inefficiencies of the people with whom he must deal, the lack of proper sanitary and hygienic conditions." And this, she says, is a manifestation of lack of concern for one's fellow man. The new *oleh* will be surprised, too, at the materialism, the social divisions and stratification and inequalities. She says, "The American *oleh* must realize that it takes time to adjust to a society which may not openly welcome him, which is fraught with inefficiencies and frustrations, and whose standards are far below those to which he has been accustomed." Now, to say that a Zionist is someone who is *en route* from New York or Toronto to Jerusalem is to ignore the fact that many people simply cannot survive that trip. One may not make a decree which the majority of the community cannot carry out. Clearly, the vast majority of the *Golah* does not suppose it can make the move. So, they are told, they cannot regard themselves as Zionists, have no share in the peoplehood of Israel.

Let the issue now be clearly drawn. There is no middle, no compromise. Either we American Zionists have an equal place in the Zionist movement or we do not. Either it is legitimate for us to pursue our own Jewish goals or it is not. The third position—that we can be Jews without Zionism—is closed to us. And so it comes down to this: either here in the *Golah* we live "good Jewish lives," or we do not. *Aliyah* simply supplies the arena for the debate of the larger issue. We do not have to give serious effort to talk of whether or not we can make a living in Israel, or whether life in America is better or worse than life in Israel. Individual preferences for a cool climate over a hot one are trivial and not pertinent to the issue. Nor are we required to claim in America's or Canada's or Britain's behalf that society is perfect and the Jews' position wholly favorable. We shall not allege Washington is our Jerusalem. The opposite is the case. What we claim is that Jerusalem is *our* Jerusalem too. The other side says it is your Jerusalem only if you live there. That seems to me a worthwhile point of debate.

At the heart of the matter is the Israelis' negation of the *Golah*. They put us in the unenviable position of having to affirm the *Golah*, when all we should like to admit is that *Golah* is *golus, but that is where we expect to remain.* Still, the *Golah* has not been a barren desert in the history of the Jewish people. Since the Israelis focus upon *Tanakh* as the central spiritual achievement of the Jewish people, it is not irrelevant to point out that the *Tanakh* as we have it is the product not of the land of Israel but of the

Babylonian Diaspora. That is to say, the Five Books of Moses, it is generally agreed by biblical scholarship, were given their present form in Babylonian Jewry in the sixth and fifth centuries B.C.E. Curiously, the Babylonian Jews placed the mark of the *Golah* on the Torah itself. They end the Torah with the death of Moses; for them, the high point in the story of the creation of the Jewish people is the revelation of the Torah—at Sinai, in no-man's-land—and not the entry of the people into the land. The Torah ends in the wilderness, on the other side of the Jordan. Now, biblical scholarship has shown that the "Five Books of Moses" really should be six, for they actually end with the story of Joshua and his conquest of the land. But the Babylonian Jews thought otherwise, and they gave us a Torah with the affirmation of the *Golah* in its very form.

Certainly, the second greatest achievement of the Jewish people is the Talmud, and I need not dwell on the point that the Talmud we study is the Babylonian one. If one then lists further enduring cultural achievements of the Jewish people, one is going to have to include medieval Hebrew poetry, the work of Spanish and Provencal Jewry; medieval Jewish philosophy, again Spanish; Jewish mysticism, the work of the *Golah* from the seventeenth century onward; Polish Hasidism and Lithuanian *yeshivah* learning; Russian writers of Hebrew literature; and German Jewish philosophy, not to mention American Jewish philanthropy and scholarship. We need not exaggerate and claim that nothing of lasting cultural value derives from the Jews in *Eretz Yisrael*. But it is the opposite of the truth to say that nothing has come out of the *Golah*. And as to the future, who knows? I for one am not ready to despair of the future of American and Canadian Jewry, because I spend my life among the young American and Canadian Jews, and know the extraordinary promise of the human materials created by our *Galuyyot*.

We therefore repudiate the form of Zionism which negates the *Golah* for three reasons.

First, because, as stated, the *Golah* has reason for pride in its past. Second, because the *Golah* has reason for hope in its future. Third, because the most difficult challenges facing world Jewry today—the challenges of materialism, of a lack of direction and purpose, of the disintegration of Jewish peoplehood in assimilation and indifference—these face Jews wherever they live, in the

State of Israel or in America or Canada or Britain or Argentina. True, when a Jew in Israel assimilates, it is into a secular society which has a Jewish veneer. But is the life of the young Israeli, indifferent to the traditions and values of Judaism, much different from the life of the equivalent young American? Both listen to the same music, wear the same clothes, dance the same dances. Both are attracted to the same politics. Both participate in the same international youth culture. Neither is closer than the other to the spiritual aspirations which have characterized the Jewish people throughout its history.

The crisis of Zionism, as Kaplan pointed out twenty years ago, is only a part of the larger crisis of Judaism. Perhaps the Israelis may rightly claim to have better means of meeting the crisis. But to the present time they do not seem to have enjoyed much greater success than we have in creating the just and righteous society the Prophets proclaimed, or in building the merciful and decent community the rabbis of the Talmud proposed, or in rooting in people's lives a sense of meaning and sacred purpose such as the Jewish philosophers and mystics discovered, or even in winning for the service of the Jewish people the loyalties and resources of ordinary people as did the Zionist movement itself.

Instead of debating whether a Zionist must live in the State of Israel, I think we had best focus discussion with Israeli Zionists on a more constructive issue. It is how to define the relationship between Zionists in various parts of the world and in the State of Israel. I hope that relationship will be marked by reciprocity, mutual respect, good will, the capacity to differ with good will and realistic mutual understanding. To be sure, we cannot describe the Israeli perception of the relationship, nor can we tell the other side how to carry on its part. But we can and should reflect upon our perception of the relationship and spell out for ourselves the potential we perceive.

First, we must recognize that that relationship provides enormous benefits to our own community. In important ways the State of Israel does for us things we cannot do for ourselves. Its society explores the potentialities of Jewishness, not to mention those of the Judaic inheritance, in ways which are closed to us. In the State of Israel we are able to understand the depths of the Judaic tradition which on our own we cannot reach.

At the same time the achievements of the State of Israel give pride to world Jewry, with our community at its head. Its accomplishments as a society and its capacity for social, cultural and political greatness attest to the character of the whole Jewish people. If all Israel stand as pledges for one another, then the State of Israel is the rightful guarantor of our good name in the world.

Second, we perceive that, just as we need the State of Israel and constant, close relationship with Israel life, so the State of Israel and its social and cultural life benefit from the ties with American Jewry. The relationship is entirely mutual and wholly reciprocal. We are their equals, as they are ours, and we can accept no other definition of the relationship.

On the material side, let us not evade the fact that now and for some time to come, the State of Israel requires the support of the Diaspora communities, American Jewry most of all. On its own resources it simply cannot do for the development of its own society what needs to be done. Moreover, the State of Israel acts in behalf of the whole Jewish people in bringing to the homeland those Jews who want or need to go there. What happens to Jews in other lands must be subordinated to those in Israel; Israel must have priority in resources, commitment, and capacities. It is the only place. It is open. It regards each Jew as precious. It wants the Jews. But without our doing our share, the State of Israel cannot carry out the task.

The State of Israel moreover requires the political support of world Jewry in gaining a hearing for its cause and in winning steady support for its security. The realities of a world of superpowers are such that American Jewry's presence and modest influence in its own country have to be regarded as nothing less than providential.

So in a worldly way, we need the State of Israel for the benefit of our own community, and the Israelis need us for their interest as well. But that relationship does not exhaust the spiritual potential of either party. For world Jewry, in important ways, the State of Israel constitutes the spiritual center, just as Ahad Ha'Am and Mordecai Kaplan said a long time ago.

What are these ways? First, the State of Israel is the greatest Jewish educational resource at hand. For us it is a classroom in Jewish living and in living Judaism, a classroom without walls. There is the best place to learn the meaning of the Sabbath. There is the place to recover our roots in our own past, the past of the Hebrew Bible and the Talmud. If we make appropriate provision for our own educational requirements, and not simply dump our young people on Israeli institutions lacking an understanding of their educational and social character, we may derive from the State of Israel educational benefits simply unavailable to any previous generation.

The State of Israel has become the spiritual center for world Jewry because it plays a decisive and central role in the Jewish mind and imagination, in shaping the Jewish identity and in the revival of the Jewish spirit in the present, not only the past generation.

But in some important ways Zionism is not enough, for it is part, not the whole, of Judaism. The State of Israel cannot serve as American Jews' "spiritual center." For being Jewish constitutes not merely a national or ethnic, cultural and social experience. It also is meant to supply an orientation toward life, a mode of being human, a perspective on man, on history, on what it means to die and to live. And those aspects of being Jewish which pertain to the nature of human existence cannot be wholly separated from the particularities of everyday life: the actual, concrete situation in which one is Jewish.

Our perception of ourselves and of the world and the meaning of life begins in our own situation, and that is a complex one. For our lives are shaped by the experience of being Jewish and being something else, many other things. We are not wholly Jewish. Our values are derived from sources other than solely Jewish or Judaic ones. Our perception of life encompasses a society quite different from that of the State of Israel. Our search for abiding values takes place in a personal and cultural setting in important ways unlike that of the State of Israel. The life for which we seek meaning, for good or ill, is a life in the *Golah,* a life in two civilizations.

We are marginal in our situation. The Israelis are at home in theirs. We are in a measure alien; they are never strangers. They perceive reality close at hand. Our perceptions are one stage removed from the center of things. For us the given is something to be criticized and elevated, for we do not take perceived reality at face value. For them things are very different. At the very center of our being is an experience unavailable to the Israeli and the contrary is also the case. Theirs is the right to criticize us and question our perpetuation of marginality. But we have made our choices, for ourselves and our children.

For us as for the Israelis there can be one common spiritual center only, and that is the Judaic tradition, which for centuries has made manifest its capacity to define and to ennoble—to sanctify—the Jewish condition under every circumstance. It is the Judaic tradition which speaks to the eternal issues of death and life, which asks questions about the purpose and meaning of existence, and which gives answers to those questions. The Judaic tradition imparts meaning to the tears and anguish of the ordinary man and woman, gives to their life transcendence, lends purpose to what seems purposeless—their living and their dying.

Judaism takes ordinary persons and shows them to be part of an extraordinary people, links them to its past and assigns them a place in its destiny, grasps hold of their private time and joins it to a rhythm of eternity, links their mortal being to the natural course of the seasons and of life itself, distinguishes one day from the next and one deed from the next. And that Judaic tradition, mediated by experience unique to a given stituation, is variously realized under all circumstances and with equal authenticity— in the *Golah* or in the Holy Land alike.

12

The Spiritual Center?
The Uses of the Circle-Metaphor

The relationship between Israeli and American Jewry is complicated by the differing ways in which each group understands itself and, consequently, the differing meanings each attaches to the language used by the other. The central problem of communication of ideas between the two groups is in the available symbols and analogies.

Common to all Israeli thought about Israel's place in world Jewry is the metaphor of the circle, with Jerusalem conceived to be the center and the *Golah* to be the periphery. One circle-metaphor, of times past, derives from Ahad Ha'Am, who spoke of the Jewish state—the *Yishuv* of his day—as "the spiritual center." Another circle-metaphor, current today, is the substantive *centrality of,* yielding "centrality of Israel" (meaning the State of Israel), or "centrality of the Land," or "centrality of Jerusalem," and similar images.

Curiously, resorting to the circle-metaphor by Israeli thinkers is partly intended to permit evasion of a quite different metaphor: *Golah* in favor of Diaspora *(tefusot),* which the *Golah* communities are imagined to prefer. Perhaps it is discourteous to look too deeply into what is intended as a courtesy, but it is time to ask whether the expression of the relationship between the two major communities of world Jewry Jewry, in the U.S. and in Israel, is well served by the circle-metaphor. Analysis of the language—

and, particularly, the analogies we use—will place on a firmer foundation the discussion of specific aspects of the relationship.

Focusing on the older of the two circle-metaphors, that of Ahad Ha'Am, we turn to one primary statement which spells out the exact substance of the "spiritual center" ("Summa Summarum," quoted from *Nationalism and the Jewish Ethic: Basic Writings of Ahad Ha'Am* [N.Y.: Schocken, 1962]):

> What has already been accomplished in Palestine [as of 1912] entitles one to say with confidence that that country will be "a national spiritual center of Judaism, to which all Jews will turn with affection, and which will bind all Jews together; a center of study and learning, of language and literature, of bodily work and spiritual purification; a true miniature of the people of Israel [meaning the Jewish people] as it ought to be . . . so that every Hebrew in the Diaspora will think it a privilege to behold just once the 'center of Judaism' and when he returns home will say to his friends: If you wish to see the genuine type of Jew, whether it be a Rabbi or a scholar or a writer, a farmer or an artist or a businessman—then go to Palestine and you will see it."

Ahad Ha'Am further held, "the whole social order . . . bears the Hebrew stamp. They do not betray, as they do in the Diaspora, traces of that foreign influence which flows from an alien environment and distorts the pure Hebrew form." And, he concludes, " . . . Here, in this country, is to be found the solution of the problem of our national existence; . . . from here the spirit shall go forth and breathe on the dry bones that are scattered east and west through all lands and all nations, and restore them to life." This, I believe, is a reliable account of what Ahad Ha'Am meant by the term "spiritual center."

Now let us turn to the contemporary use of the circle-metaphor. The position of those Israelis who take seriously communication with the *Golah* seems to be that all Jews all over the world have to acknowledge the "centrality of Israel," meaning the State of Israel, in all modes and expressions of Jewish existence. This symbol is meant to impose the judgment that living in the State makes one "a better Jew" than living abroad. To be a Zionist means to settle in the State—at a minimum (so stated Pinhas Sapir recently; I cannot report what the maximum is). All decisions pertinent to the affairs of world Jewry are to be governed by the "centrality of Israel," and to be dominated by that conviction.

It may be claimed that at issue is not symbol or metaphor, but the practical necessities facing Israelis. They need people, so have to impose upon all Jewish discourse ideas which will lead to *aliyah*. They need the lion's share of world Jewish resources, and so naturally stress the priority of the State of Israel in all practical ways. Yet, while we cannot ignore the practical foundations of the use of language and the construction of language into a picture of reality—of ideology—we should err in reducing the interpretation of the circle-metaphor to a matter of practicalities. True, Jewish leadership there and here consists of practical people who have less use for ideas than for propaganda. But there is another group of Jewish leaders, there and here, whose ideas will eventually be taken for granted by the practical leadership. Jewish intellectuals on both sides of the ocean do take ideas seriously and therefore use language with careful reflection.

Accordingly, we have to test the value of the circle-metaphor, in the two aspects before us. The first yields the conception that the State of Israel is our spiritual center. The second is that we are at the periphery of the circle of which Israelis form the center. Clearly, we have a single metaphor, in two slightly different variations.

How shall we proceed to analyze the metaphor? I can offer three approaches to analysis: accuracy, relevance, and functionality. Does the metaphor of the circle accurately describe or reflect the way things are? Is it relevant to the expression of a relationship? Does the metaphor so function as to enhance or to impede discourse? Prior to these three questions is the issue: does the metaphor fit that which it is meant to state in figurative language?

The Israeli answer is affirmative. Why? Because, living in the Land, and amply supplied with proof-texts as to its holiness, the Israeli cannot but conceive himself to be at the Jewish center. To be sure, the context and intent of the proof-texts are best ignored, for the most useful proof-texts refer to the centrality of the Land in the end of days, when the Messiah comes. Rabbi Arthur Hertzberg's analysis of how Zionism transvalued Judaic values (*The Zionist Idea* [N.Y.: Doubleday and Herzl Press, 1959]) is well known and requires no repetition. Yet when we encounter concrete instances in which eschatalogical symbols or religious values are given new meaning, we still have to remind ourselves of what Rabbi Hertzberg has taught us.

It is obvious that *qibbutz galiyyot* will take place in the eschaton, not necessarily before, and that settling in the Land, while of this-worldly value, is not what is meant in the eschatological concept. Nonetheless it jars the Jewish ear that the *Shomer Yisrael* should become anyone who purchases a $1,000 Israel Bond. The centrality of the Land and settlement in it at the end of days bear no relationship to Israel's need for a larger population today. Yet to Israelis they are identical and indistinguishable—hence, for Israelis the metaphor fits what it is meant to state; for non-Israelis it is perplexing and remarkable.

However, it is unfair to the Israelis merely to point out they are using language in a way different from its original intent. That is a trivial criticism if the language has gained for itself new and suggestive meanings. If the circle-metaphor is useful to us, as much as to them, then the expressions of that metaphor through inherited, but revised, symbols need not be limited by historical or theological considerations.

The heart of the circle-metaphor problem is that—always and everywhere—the person who uses it conceives of himself as standing at the center of the circle. How can it be otherwise? Our perception of reality begins with outselves. Our perspective is governed by our location in time and in space, our position in society, and our place in the life cycle. It is natural for each one to see himself as the beginning and the center (to mix metaphors), and it is no less natural for each group to do the same. Why should Israelis not see themselves at the center of world Jewry? On the other hand, I think it equally obvious for us to do the same.

Before us, nonetheless, are those proof-texts which tell us that Jerusalem is the center of the world, Zion is the highest mountain in the world, and the Land of Israel is the belly button of the world. I can think of no more mindless "explanation" than to hold that these sayings derive from people who lived in the city or the Land, for they were held to be true descriptions of reality by people who did not. But I can think of nothing less likely to yield an accurate interpretation of these and similar statements than to view them literally. For, if we agree that Jerusalem is the center in a literal and fundamentalist sense, then we also have to agree that

Zion is the highest mountain. Having climbed it, I can testify it is not. Fundamentalist interpretation of sacred texts can, unfortunately, be tested in empirical ways.

I have asked whether the metaphor fits that which it is meant to state in figurative language. My answer is that it does not fit the reality of people who do not live in the center of that particular circle, because they find themselves in the center of another circle of reality. They naturally perceive their mode of being as central in relationship to themselves.

Further analysis of the metaphor concerns its functionality, its relevance, and its accuracy. If the metaphor does not evoke a common perception of reality, if indeed it obfuscates, then it is obviously not functional. Secondly, the metaphor is irrelevant to people who are asked through it to interpret their own being. But what of its accuracy? Is the State of Israel "central," and are we "peripheral"?

Here we have to test the circle-metaphor against the definition supplied by the person who seems to have invented it, Ahad Ha'Am. Do the facts before us support his claims? It is impossible to argue that he spoke of some distant future, and that we have no right to measure the metaphor against everyday facts. He spoke of "what has already been accomplished...," using the present tense. We too have the right to speak of the present. Let us return to his exact language, sentence by sentence. The State of Israel most certainly *is* the place to which nearly all Jews turn with affection. But does that make it a "national spiritual center of Judaism"? If by Judaism we mean Jewish religion, broadly construed, the answer is by no means clearly in the affirmative. The State is the center of Hebrew language and literature, but its literature cannot be taken for granted as Judaic or even Jewish. Some is, some is not. And that which is, is not remarkably more evocative of the Jewish condition among our communities than that which is written here. Saul Bellow, Philip Roth, Myron Kaufman, Herbert Gold—all address themselves in varying but profound ways to the Jewish condition.

What of the State as a center of study and learning? Israel is preeminent in the study of some subjects—Hebrew language, for one, and archaeology for another. Yet, as a center of Jewish learning, it is curiously unproductive. When we consider, in particular, the actual achievements of Israeli scholars of Jewish studies who were not born in Europe, as against the actual achievements of American scholars of Jewish studies who were not born in Europe, we have to wonder at the banality and provinciality, the methodological primitivity of the Israelis from whom we have remarkably little to learn. Indeed, so many significant young American Jewish scholars have been appointed to Israeli universities in the field of Jewish studies that one must wonder: Who serves as the "spiritual center" for whom? I do not think a great many American Jews would concede that the Israeli rabbinate constitutes the "genuine Jewish type." I think the American Jewish type of rabbi would have much to contribute in the Israeli setting, in so far as it is similar to ours. I leave it to others to tell us whether Israeli businessmen are the "genuine type" of Jewish businessmen. In all, I do not think the facts will allow us to concede the accuracy of the metaphor of "spiritual center" as defined by Ahad Ha'Am. But the reason is not the failure of the State of Israel to produce on its own soil important Jewish scholarship or its inability to offer us a viable Jewish life-style which can be exported and assimilated into the American Jewish situation. The problem is deeper.

Ahad Ha'Am thought that the *Yishuv* had solved "the problem of our national existence." He claimed that the whole social order bears the Hebrew stamp and does not exhibit traces of foreign influence. As to the latter claim, it is difficult to see how Israeli everyday culture fails to betray "traces of foreign influence." There is an international life-style, charcteristic of all modernized societies, including Israel's (both the State of Israel's, and the people of Israel's) life-style. True, the Israelis use Hebrew. But what they say in Hebrew, the society they build in Hebrew, are no less a part of the international mode of life than our own, and I cannot think of anyone who would want it otherwise.

The former claim is at the very center of things, the center of the circle-metaphor: the claim of the centrality of the State and the vision of the spiritual center. *Has* the State of Israel solved "the problem of our national existence"?

The State of Israel has greatly complicated the problem of our national existence; it has also solved important problems of our national existence. No one can disagree that the Jewish people has done what it set out to do in creating a national homeland, and no one can disagree that the only way to create that homeland was by creating a state. But the state is a this-worldly, historical entity. Nothing made by mortal man finally solves any problem. It may provisionally solve one problem, but it is also apt to create others. Only if we conceive the State to be the realization of the messianic dream can we even ask whether it has finally solved "the problem of our national existence." The answer to that (unthinkable) question is self-evidently negative. In that case the presupposition of the question—the messianic idea—is shown by the facts to be not only false but either silly (to the secular mind) or blasphemous (to the religious one).

It has further to be stressed that the State of Israel is simply irrelevant to important aspects of Jewish existence—it has nothing to say about them, whether here or there. When we speak of a state, we address ourselves to a world-historical fact. That part of the existence of each of us which is engaged by the existence of all—the group, the people—is indeed affected by the world-historical fact constituted by the State of Israel. But, for most (fortunate) people most of the time, history—the events of nations and societies—is something which happens somewhere else. The perceived reality of life—the intimacies of the here and now—happen outside of history. There is a dimension of human life which endures, come what may. History and world-historical phenomena are simply not pertinent to the cycle of life, the cycle of time, the pattern of everyday doings, the sum and substance of what each of us knows as existence. That aspect of human, therefore of Jewish, existence formed by the enduring realities of daily life is scarcely touched here by what happens there. And, I think, for the private person in the State itself, the existence of the State and the nationalism which it expresses hardly encompasses all of life—though, in the present difficult circumstances they impinge upon the private existence of ordinary folk all too much.

Zionism and the State of Israel are indeed central to the world-historical existence of the Jewish people. But in so far as Jews live and suffer, are born and die, reflect and doubt, raise children and worry over them, love and work—in so far as Jews are human and live (to be sure in a most particularistic and idiomatic way) within the human condition, Zionism and the State of Israel cannot and do not form the center of their lives; indeed, they have virtually nothing to say to the enduring and eternal issues of life.

To those issues answers must be found in another place entirely. Zionism never raised the question (nor should it have raised the question) of Jewish existence as it is phrased by Judaism, and the State of Israel can hardly claim to be central to the formulation of answers to those questions.

What, then, are we to make of Ahad Ha'Am's conception of a spiritual center? So far as he claimed that the State of Israel would constitute "the center of Judaism," the very metaphors of the circle and the center are, by definition, hopelessly irrelevant. There can be no "center of Judaism," but where we find ouselves and live Jewish lives. Naturally, for the Israeli, the State of Israel is the center. But for us to say the same is not so natural at all, and contradicts the facts of our everyday life.

To begin with, how can American Jews focus their spiritual lives *solely* on a land in which they do not live? It is one thing for that land to be in heaven, at the end of time, or across the Sambatyon for that matter. It is quite another to dream of a faraway place where everything is good—*but* where we may go if we wish. The realized eschaton is insufficient for a rich and interesting fantasy life; moreover, in this-worldly terms, it is hypocritical. It means American Jews live off the capital of Israeli culture which is itself impoverished. Reliance on the State of Israel also suggests that, to satisfy their need for fantasy, American Jews must look forward to ever more romantic adventures reported in the press, rather than to the colorless times of peace. American Jews want to take their vacations among heroes, and then come home to the ordinary workaday world they enjoy, and to which Israelis rightly aspire but do not own. The "enlandisement" of American Judaism—the focusing of its imaginative, inner life upon the Land and State of Israel—thus imposes an *ersatz* spiritual dimension. We live here *as if* we lived there—but do not choose to migrate.

The issue diverts American Judaism from the concrete mythic problems it has yet to solve: Why should anyone be a *Jew* anywhere, in the U.S. or in Israel? That question is not answered by the recommendation to participate in the spiritual adventures of people in a quite different situation. Since the primary *mitzvot* of U.S. Judaism concern supplying funds, encouragement and support for Israel, one wonders whether one must be a Jew at all in order to practice that form of Judaism.

The underlying problem, which faces both Israeli and American Jews, is understanding what the ambiguous adjective *Jewish* is supposed to mean when the noun *Judaism* has been abandoned. Just what is *important* about being Jewish? In my view, the answer must pertain both to the State of Israel and to the *Golah* communities in equal measure. It cannot be right only for American Jewry, for we are not seeking a *Galut* ideology and no one would accept it. Such an ideology would obviously serve the selfish interests and the peculiar situation of American Jews alone. Nor can the answer pertain only to the situation of the Israeli Jews, for precisely the same reasons.

What is important about being Jewish is the capacity of the Jewish people and its mythic creations to preserve the tension between the intense particularities of their life and the humanity they have in common with the rest of mankind. That tension, practically unique to Jewry, derives from its exceptional historical experience. Until now, it has been the basis for the Jews' remarkable role in human history. Ahad Ha'Am claimed, and Israelis believe, that if you want to see the genuine type of Jew, then "go to the Land of Israel and you will see it." This most concrete expression of the circle-metaphor is also its refutation. For, until we have determined what we mean by "the genuine type of Jew," we cannot take out a map and see where to find it. Definitions of what is "genuine," what is a Jew, and similar long-vexed theological or ideological questions are not going to derive from propagandistic claims; they will not be imposed upon people by engines of politics and power. Rich Jews cannot purchase our minds. Political Jews cannot manipulate our hearts. For the religious Jews, theological discourse and debate, in which we do not despair of persuading one another of the rightness of our perceptions and convictions, are the only way. For the secular Jews, ideological discourse and debate are of equivalent meaning.

The Israelis make much of Masada. I believe that, had they not repudiated the whole history of the *Golah* from 70 to 1948, they would have come to a more profoundly Jewish understanding of who they are and what they have accomplished. They would have discovered the meaning of their accomplishments (and ours) not in the ultimate symbol of barren, fantastic military Messianism, *Masada*. They would have seen what to me is obvious: they are building, for themselves and for us, not *Masada* but Yavneh.

Their task is not to impose a new messianic claim in place of an old discredited one, but to seek to salvage *hasalah purta*—to save what can be saved—in the aftermath of the disaster of European Jewry.

It was they, more than we, who saved the remnants of European Jewry; it was they, more than we, who gave the Jewish people something to live, hope, and dream for. The State is the creation of European Jewry. It is the monument to European Jewry; the last, best thing we have from our common heritage in Europe. From Jerusalem to Yavneh, from Warsaw or Berlin or Amsterdam or Paris to Tel Aviv—and to Jerusalem—these seem to me, in a very simple way, parallel paths.

What did Yavneh mean in the history of the Jewish people, and in the history of Judaism? Hope beyond disaster, building in the aftermath of catastrophe, the courage to go forward against the evidence of the day. Yavneh epitomizes the Jewish people.

The State of Israel is the Yavneh of our day. That is the metaphor which, I believe, conforms to the facts; it is also wholly functional and profoundly relevant to the realities of the Jewish people. But it is a considerable task to grasp the meaning of that metaphor and to lay out its implications, for them and for us.

13

Israel and Yavneh

The Perspective of Time

How shall we understand the age in which we live? How shall we understand the place in which we live? These two questions define the grid on which we locate ourselves. The horizontal is the line of space, the vertical, the line of time. Of these two dimensions of life, it is the time in which we live which matters. It is the meaning of the *age* which determines the quality of the *place* in which we live. In a time of global war, wherever we are, we suffer. In a time of world peace, wherever we are, we prosper. "Time is the heart of existence," as Abraham Heschel says in *The Sabbath*. "Reality to us is thinghood, consisting of substances that occupy space; even God is conceived by most of us as a thing. The result of our thingness is our blindness to all reality that fails to identify itself as a thing, as a matter of fact. This is obvious in our understanding of time, which, being thingless and insubstantial, appears to us as if it had no reality."

In his later years, Heschel became deeply impressed with the holiness of place, not time, and spoke of the Wall and of Jerusalem in terms reminiscent of the way in which he described the Sabbath, our "cathedral in time." That is a measure of the age in which he wrote, of deep engagement in holy land, holy space. Indeed, I think his argument in *The Sabbath* stands at one extreme, in its stress on the centrality of the vertical line, of time, and that in *Israel: An Echo of Eternity* stands at the other, in its emphasis on the predominance of holy space, of the land.

To seek a balanced perspective on the issue, we have to look back at the history of Judaism and ask, how does Torah, under the aspect of eternity, teach us to balance the perspective of space, of holy land and the Holy Land, and the angle of vision of time, of the meaning not of land but of epoch. If we open the Bible, our attention is drawn to the holy land, the promised land, the land which is given to our forebears and to us. Surely the books assigned to Moses are about the yearning of Israel, the Jewish people, for a land of its own, a Land of Israel, its building of holy places and demarcation of holy space, its service of God in some one place. Those who argue, as does Heschel in *Israel: An Echo of Eternity,* that the definitive dimension of the sacred is one of space, of land which is holy and which is ours, find many proof-texts in scriptures. Further, students of religions recognize the universal authenticity of the biblical vision of the sacred space, for every religion speaks of its holy places, places made sacred by the divinity. If Jerusalem is the center of the world, Zion the highest hill, the Temple the umbilicus, so too for all others is there a Jerusalem, a Zion, a Temple.

But the biblical and Talmudic conception of sacred space, of the relationship of God and Israel centered upon, expressed through, the holy land, is complicated by two further ideas. First, Israel's possession of the land is conditional, not absolute. And this produces, second, the division of sacred reality not solely in terms of space, but also in terms of time. If Torah perceives time as the heart of existence, as Heschel says of the Sabbath, it is because everything is relative to the traits of the moment, of the age. Space is relative to time, not time to space. Possession of the land is conditional, not absolute, as I said, and it is conditioned upon what happens in the land—upon the traits of the epoch. Israel, after all, remembers a time before the land, endures a time without the land, recalls return to the land, hopes for yet another. Its sacred history is divided into epochs, and what makes one epoch different from another—the Deuteronomic historian makes clear—is *what* happens, not primarily *where* things happen. When, the Deuteronomist says, Israel did what was right in God's eyes, then there were good times. When Israel did not, there were troubles. What is important in this picture is that the land is the background, not the center, unlike the picture drawn by the priestly writers of Genesis, Leviticus, and Numbers, to whom the holy place is the predominant consideration, and to whom the cult in the holy place is the center of reality.

The very land-centeredness of the Torah literature as a whole, moreover, should be seen in context. The Torah literature, including the work of the Deuteronomic historians through Samuel and Kings, is the creation not of people in the land, who take the land for granted and see it—if they perceive it distinctly at all—as the backdrop, not the center of the sage, but of the exile. For the Torah literature, much of prophetic literature, and the Deuteronomic histories all are the work of the Babylonian exile, though, to be sure, the raw materials were not wholly created abroad. But the acute consciousness of land, of having land, not having land, returning to land, and of holy place and holy space—that consciousness is heightened by the experience, the age, of alienation and exile. The land is anything but a given, a datum, specifically because of the time and the place of the Torah literature: the age beyond destruction and (we now know) before restoration, on the one side, the places of exile and alienation, on the other. And this places into perspective the historic yearning of the Jewish people for its holy and promised land, a yearning made desperate by exile, made sacred by suffering, but also made fantastic by the unreal expectations attached to the land, expectations of the world to come and the messianic age which would be inaugurated by the return. In a word, at that faroff, much prayed for future, the grid would become complete: holy time and holy place made one.

It is in this perspective that I wish to interpret the problem before us, the problem of our relationship to Israel as Land and State. What I wish to do is spell out what I think is a meaningful and valid analogy, in the light of which we shall be able, I hope, to think through countless concrete questions.

First, we cannot distinguish between the Land and Israel and the State of Israel. Nothing will be gained by an unreal distinction between the Land, which is the object of our religious affections, and the State, which, we concede, requires no religious interpretation at all. Our religious tradition does not permit us such a distinction. We traditionally pray for the restoration of the people of Israel to the Land, and of the Jewish State—judges and councillors—to the Land, and of the sacrifices to the Temple—all three together and much more. We have no way of distinguishing the restoration of the people to the Land and the restoration of nationality to Israel, people and Land alike.

But does this inability to distinguish the holiness of the Land from the reality of the State of Israel not lead us into a dilemma? For if we cannot distinguish Land from State, then we also cannot explain why we do not regard as sacred the doings of the State, its politics as eschatological politics, its cabinet as our college of cardinals, its policies—whatever they are—as the will of God? Thomas Erastus, who died in 1583, gave his name to that sort of state religion. It is called Erastianism, and it holds that the state is supreme in religious affairs. But it was not until the twentieth century that Erastianism was given a really bad name, that the worship of the state was accorded religious priority. The Führer and his will, the state and its symbols, showed what Erastianism meant. And we in America, whose free institutions survived a sustained and powerful assault by lawless men in high positions of power, have no use for the deification of the state, for the imperial presidency, for the identification of the will of the president with the will of God. Statism, whether cloaked with classical religious garments or hidden in the mask of nationalism, is not only the enemy of democracy and human freedom, it is also a heresy against God and Torah. Whether the state held to be sacred is Germany, America, Russia or the State of Israel, does not matter. The state is contingent. It is the work of mortal men and women. We cannot accord it sanctity or holiness, regard its welfare—let alone the convenience of the ruling party—as a predominant consideration, but only as relative.

This exposes the dilemma which Jews face. We cannot, as I said, distinguish the sanctity of the Land from the State which our people have built upon the land. And we also cannot accord to the State the status of the sacred at all.

If this were merely a theoretical dilemma, I should not trouble Israel to think about it. But it is hardly theoretical. We are privileged to live in the era in which the Jewish people has created a state. That state came into being as a direct consequence of the annihilation of one-third of our people. It comes to us as a miracle, as consolation, as a day which God has made in which we rejoice. For many among us, moreover, the State of Israel is conceived in a spatial and geographical sense to be the center of the Jewish people, in a cultural or religious sense to be the spiritual center of the Jewish people. That is why "platforms" are built in Jerusalem upon the plank of "the centrality of Israel," meaning of the State of Israel. That is why we who choose to live in the Diaspora are asked to feel guilty about our choice, are endowed with second-class citizenship in the polity of the Jewish people, are instructed to listen and not to speak, to contribute but not to take or to ask where our money goes. There are many in our communities who hold that the only worthwhile thing we do as Jews is support the State of Israel, the only thing we should do as Jews is give money and raise our children to settle there.

Those people take up a position I call "Israelism," in that they make the State of Israel into the central interpretive principle by which they view Jewish realities—the Jewish people and Judaism. All of Jewish history has been leading to this place, this holy space. The return to Zion of which the prophets spoke has now been realized. If the Messiah has not come, the Messiah is coming very soon, and the messianic cataclysm is upon us. Viewed in the dimension of space, the Israelists have a powerful claim upon our minds, just as their sense of the situation appeals to our emotions and our reason. They hold that the "Jewish problem" has been solved. If they are religious—and the majority of the religious politicians in the State of Israel seem to take this position—then they hold that the realization of the prophets' and sages' promises, promises of the Land and redemption, is before us. That is why, in concrete terms, our side must hold on to all that was "Israel" in ancient times, the whole of the promised land. For now the promises are being kept. And it is our task to keep them, as much as it is God's task to keep them. The Israelists among us, as I said naturally take the position that nothing we do is worthwhile, except when it has to do with the Land and State of Israel. The task of the Diaspora is to dissolve itself—and, at the very least, to deny its own integrity and legitimacy within the Jewish polity. They give us a radical answer to the question of how shall we understand the place in which we live? The Israelist answer is, unless we live in the holy land, we live in a diminished reality. We live without God and Torah, for God and Torah are in the holy land. To them, in Heschel's terms, "reality is thinghood."

In defense of Israelism, let us observe how deeply it appeals to the hurt and anguish of the Jewish people. For it is a negation of all that is negative: exile, alienation, to be sure, but also annihilation, gas chambers built by the world, to hasten the self-annihilation begun in our homes through dejudaization. Israelism promises a final solution to the Jewish problem, a solution of land, state, strength, a future, freedom from the gentiles and their opinions, freedom to do as we like, freedom, at least, to die like other men and women, and not like sheep. I doubt that any Jew is immune to the profound, existential appeal of this messianic conception of the world, this centering upon place and space for the discovery of where we stand in the grid of eternity, of where we go. What a sense of remission, of relief, it is to conceive in such decisive and spatial terms the meaning of our fate and the promise of our destiny: How natural to the Diaspora, in particular, is it to seek the lines of order and of meaning in the organization of space, in the interpretation of time in terms of the dimensions of land and holy place: Like the priestly redactors of the Torah books and the Deuteronomic redactors of the histories of ancient Israel, we clearly perceive the meaning of space and of distance from the promised land—that "downtown," where "everything's great when you're downtown," that eschaton of land! How comforting it is for us who are aware of the promise of destruction contained in our history among the nations to think that out there, somewhere, is a history free of the nations, a place of ultimate rest, of permanent security, uncontingent peace, forever and ever, world without end.

I do not condemn Israelism—messianic, Erastian, fantastic though it is. It is simply a religious option I cannot espouse. Like an atheist viewing religious people, I respect the sincerity and marvel at the capacity of people to be so wrong, to believe that their dreams are real, to confuse fantasy with reality. For Israelism makes claims about eternity which we may test in time. Has history ended? Has the Jewish problem been solved? Are we now free of the nations? Can we determine our own fate? Have our judges been restored "as of old" and are the sacred offerings made once again? Is it to this we have come, for which we pray and hope? I think not. I hope not.

But that is not the end of the matter, only the beginning. For if we do not see the State of Israel as the harbinger of the Messiah, if we do not regard the government in Jerusalem as better than the government in Washington, if we do not imagine that the Jewish people has reached the rest and solace of freedom from the opinions and power of the nations, then how do we understand the world? How do we interpret the age in which we live and the place in which we live? If the State of Israel does not mean what the Israelists say it means, then how shall we go about proposing an alternative view?

The answer lies in the alternative on the grid, the line of time. Let us seek an understanding of Jewish existence which draws lines of demarcation (so to speak) in terms of the era or the epoch, an age which all Jewry, in the Land and in the exile, share as one. To illustrate, let us begin with a small matter, the concept of exile. Clearly, for those who see reality spatially, exile is everywhere outside the Land. But for those who see reality in terms of temporal nuance, exile is a condition, a set of qualities, which may be found anywhere, abroad or in the Land. When we are told that God's spirit is in exile, is the exile spatial? Is God's spirit then a thing, with a place? Or do we speak of profound spiritual mysteries, of an exile which is brought about by a tragic ontological flaw in the very being of reality? Is exile not at least as much a state of mind, a sense of alienation from oneself and one's authentic being, as it is a state of location? Why is it that being in the Land is the end of exile? Not because one is in a different place, I think, but because being in the the Land creates a reality in which we find ourselves at home, at one.

I do not maintain that exile is a category of time, not space. I maintain that exile is a category of time *and* space. Ours is not a spiritual and unworldly being, a life *as if,* but a life which is *as if* and which also is here and now. Accordingly, we cannot say that exile is so spiritual, so unreal and unconcrete an experience, that it can take place anywhere, with the necessary consequence that the Land too is "anywhere we feel ourselves at home," at one. Diaspora is exile, here. The holy land is a specific place. But exile is two-dimensional, an aspect of space, but also an aspect of time, of the age in which we live.

This simple, self-evident example now permits us to turn to the complicated problem of interpreting our existence in relationship to the State of Israel. As I said, we seek a temporal interpretation, a way of understanding and appreciating the age in which all Israel, the whole Jewish people, find themselves. We seek, therefore, to define not what is the spatial or geographical center of our lives, as we should if our primary analogy were drawn from space, but what are the temporal and epochal traits of our lives. For our primary analogy is borrowed from history and is meant to point toward eternity.

Where are we in time? How do we differentiate this time from some other?

Let us try to describe our age by its largest and most encompassing traits. First, this is a time of surviving. We all are brands plucked from the burning. Second, this is a time of rebuilding. The lives of all of us have been touched by troubles. We all have to construct a capacity to live beyond the damning gnosis of holocaust. Third, this is a time of affirmation of Israel, the Jewish people, not only against the destroyers of the past, but against the enemies of the present. Just as Pharaoh told us not to have children, so Fahmi tells us not to have children, not to populate the Land.

In this time of desperation, of untold danger, of crisis which is at once chronic and acute, we live, in a single moment, the whole of Jewish history. For when have the Jewish people known peace? When have we known we could look forward to years, to centuries, of security in the lands of our habitation? The age in which we live is the single moment, a single hour, in which all Jews have lived from the end of the holy Temple and in which all Jews will live until the Messiah comes: an age of risk and ruin, of moderated hope and calculated chance, a time which calls for probity and caution, judiciousness and sane concern, not panic, not complacency.

Yet it is not wholly like those long Jewish centuries from 70 to 1948, because of what happened 1948 and what continues to happen to this hour: the advent of an act of Jewish daring and defiance, an act of spite in the face of history, the making of the Jewish state in the holy Land. If I argue that the State of Israel is not our spiritual center because geographical and spatial analogues do not serve, that is not to suggest nothing has changed. On the contrary, no analogy is possible which does not take account of the ineffable fact that, for once and at last, there is a refuge and a bastion for our people.

In the long sequence of time, of age upon age, one time does differ from another, even though all find a place within the largely undifferentiated continuum of unredemption. And what differentiates our age from the eras that lie behind us is the presence of the State of Israel, the promise of the State, but, above all, the challenge of the State. Curiously, we who are among the smallest and the weakest peoples of the world find ourselves precisely where the prophets and apocalyptists of old saw us, which is at the center of the stage of history and at the focus of human destiny. It is an embarrassing and troubling thought, and, if we could say it, we might not hesitate to wonder whether it is also the intent of God. For Israel, bearer of redemption of humankind, makes its way through time unending, as God promised so long ago to the prophets and as the apocalyptists foresaw. We who in our own day are the "afflicted, storm-tossed and not comforted," we bear witness to this truth: "For the mountains may depart, and the hills be removed, but my steadfast love shall not depart from you, and my covenant of peace shall not be removed, says the Lord who has compassion on you." I see in the age begun in 1933 and come to climax in 1948, and continuing to this day evidence that, though afflicted, we are the people whom God loves steadfastly and with whom the covenant of peace endures.

But more: Let us ask about a still more concrete analogy, a specific moment in the history of the Jewish people to which we compare our own day, through which we may understand the age in which we live. That time comes with the destruction of the Second Temple, the end of the sacred cult, inaugurated by God through Moses in the wilderness (to speak in the language of biblical myth). The destruction marked the utter disorientation of the Jews, for the place from which the lines of structure and organization, both social and cosmic, had radiated was no more. What now is sacred? What takes the place the Temple once held? What now stands at the center of things?

The rabbis of Yavneh answered that question. What now is holy is the *people* of Israel, whose life is set apart and sacred as was the life of the Temple, whose life is the life of sacrifice. To take one trivial illustration of this cosmic conception, the rabbis after 70 held that "leprosy" was caused by arrogance or gossip. What does that mean? "Leprosy" was a disease which kept a person out of the Temple. To say it is caused by gossip, we now claim that a person who commits a sin against the community is kept out of the community, just as a person who was a "leper" was kept out of the Temple. And the reason is that the community, the Jewish people, now is sacred as is the Temple. The rabbis who survived the destruction of the Temple preserved but took over into their system the wide range of Temple symbols and rites. Study of Torah is the new mode of sacrifice. The rabbi is the new priest. Deeds of loving kindness are the new freewill offerings. And, it follows, the community formed on the basis of the rabbis' Torah, the Jewish people, also is going to be protected from social uncleanness, just as the old Temple was protected from cultic uncleanness. True, the Temple is destroyed, and we hope and pray it will be restored. But Israel, the Jewish people, is now the Temple, or, to put it differently, in the new age, it is Israel which must serve as surrogate for the holy place. It is the life of Israel which must take the place of the ancient cult. The covenant now is represented by the people with whom the covenant was made.

In this age in which we live, an age of darkness illumined by the light of Zion, we seek no spatial center for our spiritual life, but a conception of time, of the meaning of the age. That meaning I derive from the endurance of the Jewish people, its importance in the history of the nations, its capacity to go onward and forward through time. It is this pilgrim people, moving through the wilderness, purified by the suffering of the desert, which we are, all together. In the line of time, it is the peoplehood of Israel that endows all else with nuance and meaning. The State is important because it is the State of *Israel,* because it serves the spiritual and material welfare of the Jewish people. The *State* is not central, though it is important. It is not predominant, though it is significant. It is Israel which is central, it is Israel which is, in the context of Judaism, predominant. The *State* of Israel is just that, contingent, useful, serving valuable ends. The *people of Israel* is uncontingent, absolute, more than merely useful. The State is the means to an end. The end is determined by the Jewish people.

Yet we have need to dwell upon the meaning of that people, formed as it is in the covenant with God, established as it is through Torah. "Only you have I known of all the families of man. Therefore I shall visit upon you all your iniquities." Our suffering testifies to God's knowledge of us. Our importance in world history, our disproportionate role and place in the center of the stage of world history—these testify not to our importance but to God's name, by which we are called. It is Israel of whom the prophet spoke, and it is as if he spoke to this very moment, to a time of the power of our enemies, the great powers of the world, Russia, China, the Arab world, assembled in General Assembly, powers fearful to allow us to speak, powers who carry on the work of Hitler: "by oppression and judgment he was taken away, and as for his generation, who considered that he was cut off out of the land of the living? For we bear the sin of many, yet make intercession for the transgressors. Upon us is the suffering that makes mankind whole." God has made us suffer for, and bear the weight of, the sinful deeds of mankind. We are despised and rejected by men, we are a people of sorrows and acquainted with grief. We are those from whom the nations hid and hide their faces. We are despised, and we are not esteemed. We bear the griefs and carry the sorrows of the nations. This I take to be the meaning of the present moment.

And who stands forth among Israel, who represents Israel, the Jewish people, if not the State of Israel? If, as I said, in this age of destruction and rebuilding, we seek to understand who we are, and what is between us and Zion—*mah lanu velesiyyon*—there is our answer: of all Israel, the Jewish people, there stands forth as the suffering servant of Isaiah, that State, the State of *Israel*. Is this not enough, that the State should be the Jewish state, the State of *Israel*? Do we have to concede it is the messianic state as well? I think not.

Dayyo lavo min hadin lihyot kenidon. Let me paraphrase that Talmudic principle of logic: It is sufficient that that which comes forth in judgment represent, stand for, all who are judged. In the age of Yavneh, of destruction and reconstruction, there is a place which is like the vineyard of Yavneh, a place to which we turn for Torah, and which, some day if not now, may be worthy of our commitment and attention.

Summing Up

*Zionism, "The Jewish Problem"
and Judaism*

The issue of this discussion is not Zionism, let alone "the Holocaust," but Judaism. For whether or not there can be a form of Zionism relevant to the ordinary lives of American Jews, there certainly is a form of Judaism. It is that Judaism which in the end is the one significant human achievement of American Jews. The painful dilemmas outlined in preceding parts therefore confront not only American Jews but also American Judaism. For Zionism imposes its judgments not only upon where people live but also upon the meaning of their ancient heritage. Zionism, after all, rewrites the meaning of the Judaic vocabulary. It rereads the world created by the Judaic myth, as much as it reworks chosen elements of that myth. In so far as Zionism is more than merely a political movement for the saving of lives of Jews in danger but a statement of, a judgment upon, the meaning of Judaism, Zionism poses a considerable dilemma to the distinctive adaptations and expressions of Judaism, as much as to the Jews, of America.

The first paper here, "Judaism and the Zionist Problem," spells out the substance of this problem and proposes its solution. It takes up the challenge encapsulated in the word *enlandisement*, that is to say, the imposition upon Judaism, a universal religion, of its old-new tie to a particular place, the locativism of Zionism. In the tension between the locative and the utopian, Zionism comes perilously close, after all, to resolving the tension in favor of place, with consequences now amply spelled out. Yet if we reframe the tension, it may be stated also as the conflict not between place and no-place, but between people and no-people. That is to say the tension is between "the particular" and "the universal" in that locative-utopian thing, Judaism. Stated in this way, the question becomes the one I raised in the introduction: how to frame a Judaism around experienced reality? For now we perceive a Judaism for Jews which is like ballet choreographed for clumsy oafs; a system of salvation by others for others; an existential counterpart to sports as spectacles, not as exercise, not for fun. Once we see matters with the help of the stated simile and metaphors, the question confronts Israeli Judaism as much as it does American Judaism, if along different lines entirely. In the end the answer is the very affirmation of the generative power and force of the question. These points of tension between place and no-place, people and no-people, define all there is, and all (God willing) there ever will be. Judaism in its American-Judaic formulation calls for love with a breaking heart, holding close with open arms. It is the people, one people, which mends the broken heart and draws the open arms into closed embrace.

For the costs of Zionism, so painfully toted up in these pages, are to be balanced against the gains. There is, after all, the State, with its Jewish way of life, its Hebrew language, and, in our context of discourse, its remarkable presence and evocative power in the imagination of American Jewry. There is, again, that particular reading of the "Jewish problem," solved now and (God willing) for all time to come by the Jewish state. These are not nothing. Against such gains, it is hard to find weighty the costs of paradox, contradiction, and, alas, recognition of one's self-deception and inner contradiction nearing hypocrisy.

In the last paper, "Zionism and 'The Jewish Problem,'" I take up this "Jewish problem" addressed so routinely in the last century and raised so seldom in this one. There are three Jewish problems solved by Zionism: the crisis of identity, the liberal dilemma, and, the point at which we began, the problem of self-hatred. Here I try to explain how I believe Zionism confronts and resolves these problems. Because Zionism solves "the Jewish problem" as I have spelled it out, Zionism takes that central place in the definition of American Judaism which has occupied us for so many pages.

14

Judaism and the Zionist Problem

The success of Zionism in solving the central Jewish problems of the modern age also creates new dilemmas for the Judaic religious tradition. Since Zionism functions for Jewry in much the same way as religions do for other peoples, the role and function of *Judaism*—the complex of myths, rituals, social and cultural forms by which classical Jews experienced and interpreted reality—now prove exceptionally ambiguous. Because Zionism appropriates the eschatological language and symbolism of classical Judaism, Judaists face an unwanted alternative: either to repudiate Zionism or to acquiesce in the historicization, the politicization, of what had formerly stood above politics and beyond history. The choice to be sure was recognized and faced by small Reform and Orthodox circles, as everyone knows. The classical reformers repudiated Zionism in the name of the mission of Israel, which, they held, required Jewry to take a decisive role in the universal achievement by all men of the messianic age. Their last, and unworthy, heirs accurately repeat the rhetoric, but do not possess the moral authority, of the nineteenth-century reformers. Likewise, Orthodox leadership in Eastern Europe and the U.S.A. quite early discerned what they understood to be the heretical tendency of Zionism: the advocacy that Jews save themselves, rather than depend on the Messiah, and return to Zion before the foreordained end of time. Their repulsive continuators present no interesting differences from the anti-Zionist reformers.

171

For the great mass of American Jews, who take literally the Zionist interpretation of Jewish history and innocently identify Zionism with Judaism, but regard themselves also both as Americans by nationality and Jews by religion, naive belief substitutes for and precludes close analysis. They have yet to come to grips with the inner contradictions recognized by the extremists of Reform and Orthodox Judaism. Indeed, they exasperate Israeli Zionists as much as Diaspora anti-Zionists. If Zionist, then why American? If the end has come, why not accept the discipline of the eschaton? If the end has not come, how to justify the revision of the Judaic consciousness and its reformation along Zionist lines? Nor has U.S. Jewry taken seriously the demands of logic and intellect for the formation of a credible ideology to explain the status quo and justify it.

But the problem is not American alone, nor does it face only those who articulately espouse the Zionist idea. And, rightly understood, the problem is not a new one. The tension between ethnicism and religion, between "enlandisement" and universality, between Jewish nationalism and the mission of Israel, characterizes the history of the Jewish people and of Judaism throughout. Take, for example, the conflict of symbolism represented by Torah and Messiah. One achieves salvation through study of Torah and carrying out its precepts. *Or* one will be saved at the end of days by the Messiah of the House of David. But if Messiah, what need of Torah? And if Torah, why the Messiah? To be sure, the two are harmonized: If all Israel will keep a single Sabbath as the Torah teaches, then the Messiah will come. So the one is made to depend on the other. For the Talmudic rabbis, the Messiah depends upon Torah, and is therefore subordinate. Torah is an essentially particularist means of attaining salvation. Its observance is the obligation of Jews. Of all the commandments therein, only seven apply to non-Jews. The Messiah is primarily a universal figure. His action affects all mankind. Both nature and the nations, as much as Israel and its Land, are the objects of his solicitude. Israel first, to be sure, but everyone at last comes to the end of days.

The tension between *holy land* and *holy Torah* as salvific symbols is pointed out by 'Abd al-Tafāhum in a remarkable essay, "Doctrine," (in A. J. Arberry, ed., *Religion in the Middle East* [Cambridge, 1969], vol. 2, pt. 2: *The Three Religions in Concord and Conflict*). What is remarkable is that al-Tafāhum (who is, I presume, a Moslem, though he is not identified by the editor) writes informedly and sympathetically about all three Middle Eastern religions. He writes (p. 367), "The whole self-understanding of the Hebrews turns on 'enlandisement' and habitation and then, centuries later, on 'disenlandisement' and dispersion. Its two poles are Exodus and Exile. . . . The triangular relationship is that of God, people, and territory."

With the Exile, the physical symbol is reenforced, and, in time, moved into the framework of the last things. Internalizing the effects of historical weakness, the Jews understood the exile as punishment for their sins in the Land—"unrighteous tenancy"—and, as al-Tafāhum says, "The single theme of 'enlandisement' as the sign and pledge of the divine will and the human response" becomes paramount. To this is added a second understanding of Exile: "the nationhood to educate nations, the awareness of election and particularity that embraces a universal parable for all the segments of mankind and all the diversified economic and spiritual tenancies of terrestrial habitation by peoples and races in those interactions that make culture and history."

The meaning of Jewish history therefore becomes the philosophy of "experienced Zion"—an experience available both in the Land and outside of it. The symbolism of Judaic religious experience was ever more shaped by having *and* not having the Land. Having the Land means standing in a proper relationship with the natural order. Al-Tafāhum refers to A. D. Gordon: "everything creaturely is material for sanctification . . . The land of promise is properly not merely a divine bestowal but human fulfilment." Love of Zion produces the marriage of Messiahship and kingship, land and nation. Above all, it bears the intense particularities of Jewish existence, the overwhelming love for Israel—Land, people, faith—characteristic of Jews through time.

"Disenlandisement," by contrast, produces the universal concern of Israel for all people: the willingness to enter into intimate relationship with each and every civilization. Election stands over against universality, but not wholly so: "Only you have I known among the families of man, therefore I shall visit on you all your iniquities." The unresolved tension in the history of Judaism is between privilege and particularity, on the one side, and the privilege of service to men on the other. Unlike Christianity, Judaism never chose to transcend its history, its intimacy with the Jews.

Al-Tafāhum poses the question: "If Jewry disapproves the universalizing of its human mission which has happened in the Church, how does it continue to reconcile its sense of privilege with the self-transcending obligation, confessed and prized, within that very identity?" Is Israel, the Jewish people, a mere ethnic continuity? Can it equate spiritual vocation with biological persistence? "Can the 'seed of Abraham' in any case be, in these times, a physically guaranteed notion? Is destiny identical with heredity and fidelity with birth?" "Can [Jewry] either delegate its universal duty or realize it merely by the percentage of literal seed?"

In former times, these questions found a response in the allegation that Israel had a mission to carry out among the nations. Israel was a presence within the world, "absorbing its values, using its languages and participating in its life, while casting off, sometimes almost in embarrassment, the distinctiveness of its own history and cultic life." But that response has its limitations, for in discounting the "historic elements of dogma and sanctity," Jews lost also all sense of particularity and readily gave up what was unique to themselves to join the commonalities of mankind. The mission ended in assimilation among those to be missionized.

Zionism, al-Tafāhum observes, "posits in new and more incisive form the old question of universality." It contains within itself "an ever sharper ambiguity about the final questions of the universal meaning and obligation of the chosen people. . . . By its own deepest convictions Judaism is committed to the benediction of all people and without this loyalty its very particularity is disqualified."

The question therefore stands: "Has the new 'enlandisement' betrayed the old? Was Diaspora the true symbol or the tragic negation of what vocation meant? Are chosen-ness and the law, identity as God's and duty to man, still proper and feasible clues to Jewish existence? Or is the land now no more than the territorial location of a secular nationality apostate from itself?" Al-Tafāhum rightly asserts that these issues are not of merely political interest, for "they reach most deeply into . . . the doctrinal heart." It would be difficult to improve upon this statement of the dilemma raised for modern Judaism by Zionism. If Zionism solves "the Jewish problem," it also creates interesting problems for Judaism.

Jews, too, have recognized this paradoxical quality of Jewish existence, amid a universal, international situation. Writing in *The New Yorker* (March 21, 1970), I. B. Singer has a character state,

> The modern Jew can't live without anti-Semitism. If it's not there, he's driven to create it. He has to bleed for humanity—battle the reactionaries, worry about the Chinese, the Manchurians, the Russians, the untouchables in India, the Negroes in America. He preaches revolution and at the same time he wants all the privileges of capitalism for himself. He tries to destroy nationalism in others but prides himself on belonging to the Chosen People. How can a tribe like this exist among strangers...

One can hardly regard Singer's insight as mere fiction, when the Lakeville studies have shown it is fact.

There, suburban Jews, studied by Marshall Sklare and Joseph Greenblum (*Jewish Identity on the Suburban Frontier* [N.Y., 1967]), raise Jewish children in a culture of equalitarianism and send them to colleges where ethnic liberalism predominates. At the same time they expect the children to develop strong Jewish identification. To be a good Jew in Lakeville is to be ethical, kind, helpful. But moral excellence does not derive from the particular ethic of Judaism, though people suppose it does. It is a function of the generalized upper-class liberalism of the community.

The authors wonder, "Will not a sectarianism which is unsupported ideologically wither away when social conditions change? Will future generations be prepared to live with the dichotomy which the Lakeville Jew abides: a universal humanitarianism as the prime value in combination with the practice of giving priority to Jewish causes? May [future generations] not conclude that their humanitarian aspirations dictate that they place the accent on the general rather than the Jewish?"

The paradox expressed by Singer accurately describes Lakeville Jews, who espouse universal values and teach them to their children, while at the same time wanting to preserve their own particular group, to marry their children off only to Jews. If the people is unique, then what is universal about it? If the people wish to preserve its ethnic existence, then why should it claim to stand with, and for, all mankind?

Zionism solves "the Jewish problem." Its success lies only partially in politics. The more profound problems for which it serves as a satisfactory solution are inward, spiritual, and, ultimately, religious. Just as the Judaic tradition had formerly told Jews what it meant to be Jewish—had supplied them with a considerable definition of their identity—so does Zionism in the modern age. Jews who had lost hold of the mythic structure of the past were given a grasp on a new myth, one composed of the restructured remnants of the old one.

The Jew had formerly been a member of a religious nation, believing in Torah revealed at Sinai, in one God who had chosen Israel, hoping for the Messiah and return to the Land in the end of days. Jews who gave up that story of where they came from and who they are tell a new story based on the old, but in superficially secular form. To be Jewish means to live in the Land and share in the life of the Jewish nation, which became the State of Israel.

To a hostile observer, things looked like this: the elements of "Jewishness" and the components of "Israelism" are to be one and the same—sacrifice, regeneration, resurrection. The sacrifice is no longer in the Temple; no prophets need decry the multitudes of fatted beasts. What now must be sacrificed is the blood of Israelis and the treasure of the Diaspora. The regeneration is no longer to be the turning of sinners to repentence—*teshuvah*—but rather the reformation of the economic and cultural realities of the Jewish people. No longer "parasites," but farmers, no longer dependent upon the cultural achievements of the nations but creators of a Hebrew, and "enlandised," culture, the Jews would be reborn into a new being and a new age. The resurrection is no longer of the dead at the end of time, but of the people at the end of the Holocaust.

The unfriendly witness sees matters this way: The new Zionist identity, like the old Judaic one, supplied a law for the rituals and attitudes of the faith. The old *halakhah* was made irrelevant, the object of party politics. The new was not partisan at all. All believed in, all fulfilled the law, except for sinners and heretics beyond the pale. The new law requires of Jewish men and women one great commandment: support Israel. Those who do it best, live there. Those who do not, pay a costly atonement in guilt and ransom for the absent body. The ransom is paid through the perpetual mobilization of the community in an unending campaign for funds. The guilt is exorcised through political rituals: letters to Congressmen and—for bourgeois Jews, what would normally be unheard of—mass rallies and street demonstrations. The guilt of Auschwitz and the sin of living in the Diaspora become intertwined: "On account of our sin do we live today, and in the wrong place at that!" Above all, the guilty and the sinner forever atone by turning to the *qiblah* of the Land: There is no Land but Israel, and the Jewish people are its product. The development of an American Jewish, or Judaic, culture is seen as irrelevant to the faith. The philanthropists will not support it, for no funds are left after allocations for Israel and for domestic humanitarian institutions. The rabbis will not speak of it, for the people will not listen. The people will hear of nothing but victories, and victories are won in this world, upon a fleshly battlefield, with weapons of war.

The old self-hatred—the vile anti-Semitism of an Alexander Portnoy—is left behind. No longer weak, one hardly needs to compensate for weakness by pretensions to moral superiority, and then to pay the price of that compensation by hatred of one's own weakness. Jews no longer look down on *goyim*, for they feel like them. The universal humanism, the cosmopolitanism of the old Jew are abandoned in the new particularism. The old grandmother who looked for Jewish names in reports of plane crashes has given way to the new grandson who turns off the news after the Middle Eastern reports are done with.

The Jews no longer make contradictory demands on society. They no longer want to be accepted into the tradition of society. In the new ethnicism of the hour, they seek only their share. The liberal dilemma has been resolved. Jews now quite honestly' interpret the universe in terms of their particular concerns. Self-hatred, liberalism, the crisis of identity—the three characteristics of the mid-twentieth-century American Jew—all fade into the background. The end of the old myths no longer matters much, for new ones have arisen in their place. The American Jews who did not want to be so Jewish that they could not also be part of the undifferentiated majority have had their wish fulfilled. Some have indeed ceased to be Jewish at all, and no one cares. Many others have found a place in the new, well-differentiated majority—so goes the hostile view.

In my view, it is reactionary to cavil at these developments. Only an antiquarian cares about the end of old myths and the solution of the dilemmas that followed. Zionists need make no apologies to those who point out the profound changes Zionism effects in Jewish existence. They need only ask, Is self-hatred better than what we have done? Is a crisis of identity to be preferred over its resolution? Are people better off living among the remnants of disappointed otherworldly hopes, or shaping new aspirations? Surely it is healthier to recover a normal life than to lament the end of an abnormal one. Granted that the Jewish situation has radically changed, I contend it is no worse, and a good deal better, than what has been left behind. All the invidious contrasts in the world change nothing.

Zionism has had a uniformly beneficial effect upon Jewry. It achieves the reconstruction of Jewish identity by its reaffirmation of the nationhood of Israel in the face of the disintegration of the religious foundations of Jewish peoplehood. Zionism indeed supplies a satisfactory explanation for the continued life of the Jewish group. It reintegrates the realities of Jewish group life with an emotional, intellectual, and mythic explanation for those realities. If Zionism really is a new religion for the Jews, then I think, on that account, it is not obligated to apologize for its success. On the contrary, Zionism works a miracle by making it possible for the Jewish group to renew its life. It redeems the broken lives of the remnants of the Holocaust. But it also breathes new life into the survivors of a different sort of holocaust, the erosion of Jewish self-respect, dignity, and loyalty throughout the Western Diaspora. Jews who want more than anything else to become Americans are enabled to reaffirm their Jewishness. Throughout the world, Jews who had lost a religious, Judaic way of viewing reality regain a Jewish understanding of themselves.

Zionism indeed serves as a religion because it does what a religion must do: it supplies the meaning of felt history; it explains reality, makes sense of chaos, and supplies a worthwhile dream for people who find in Jewishness nothing more than neurotic nightmares. Neither metaphysics nor theology proves necessary, for Zionism explains what the people already know and take for granted as fact. Zionism legitimates what Alexander Portnoy observed but could not accept: that Jews are men of flesh and blood, that (in Portnoy's phrase), *there is an id in Yid.* What is remarkable is that the early Zionists sought to do just that: to normalize the existence of the Jewish people.

In what way, then, does Zionism constitute a problem for Judaism? In my view, it is not its secularity and worldliness, but the mythic insufficiency of Zionism that renders its success a dilemma for contemporary American Jews, and for Israeli ones as well. To be sure, for some Israelis and American Jews, to be a Jew is to be a citizen of the State of Israel—but that definition hardly serves when Israeli Moslems and Christians are taken into account. If one ignores the exceptions, the rule is still wanting. If to be a Jew is to be—or to dream of being—an Israeli, then the Israeli who chooses to settle in a foreign country ceases to be a Jew on giving up Israeli citizenship for some other. If all Jews are on the road to Zion, then those who either do not get there or, once there, choose another way are to be abandoned. That makes Jewishness depend upon quite worldly issues: This one cannot make his living in Tel Aviv, that one does not like the climate of Afula, the other is frustrated by the bureaucracy of Jerusalem. Are they then supposed to give up their share in the "God of Israel"?

More seriously still, the complete "enlandisement" of Judaism for the first time since 586 B.C.E. forces the Judaic tradition to depend upon the historical fortunes of a single population in a small country. The chances for the survival of the Jewish people have surely been enhanced by the dispersion of the Jews among differing political systems. Until World War II Jews had stood on both sides of every international contest from most remote antiquity. Now, we enter an age in which the fate of Jewry and destiny of Judaism are supposed to depend on the fortunes of one state and one community alone.

That, to be sure, is not a fact, for even now the great Jewish communities in the U.S.S.R., Western Europe, Latin America, and North America, as well as smaller ones elsewhere, continue to conform to the historical pattern. But, ideologically, things have vastly changed. With all the Jewish eggs in one basket, the consequence of military actions is supposed to determine the future of the whole of Jewry and Judaism. So the excellence of some eight hundred pilots and the availability of a few dozen fighter bombers are what it all comes down to. Instead of the thirty-six righteous men of classical myth are seventy-two Phantoms—Mirages—a curious revision of the old symbolism.

Just what is *important* about being Jewish and in Judaism? In my view, the answer must pertain both to the State of Israel and to the *Golah* communities in equal measure. It cannot be right only for American Jewry, for we are not seeking a *Galut* ideology and no one would accept it. Such an ideology—right for here but irrelevant to Israelis—would obviously serve the selfish interests and the peculiar situation of American Jews alone. But the answer cannot pertain only to the situation of the Israeli Jews, for precisely the same reasons.

What is important about being Jewish is the capacity of the Jewish people and its mythic creations to preserve the tension between the intense particularities of their life and the humanity they have in common with the rest of mankind. That tension, practically unique to Jewry, derives from its exceptional historical experience. Until now, it has been the basis for the Jews' remarkable role in human history.

Others have not felt such a tension. To be human and to be English—or Navaho—were hardly differentiated. And why should they have been, when pretty much everyone one cared for and knew was English, or Navaho? To be a Jew in any civilization was, and is, to share the values held by everyone *but* to stand in some ways apart from (not above) the others. It was, and is, to love one's native land with open arms, to preserve the awareness of other ways of living life and shaping culture.

To be sure, before the destruction of the First Temple, Jewish people may well have been much like others. But from that time forward the Land was loved with an uncommon intensity, for it had been lost, then regained, therefore could never again be taken for granted. And alongside land, the people found, as few have *had* to, that Jews live by truths that could endure outside a single land and culture. Jewry discovered in itself an international culture, to be created and recreated in every land and in every language. It found in its central moral and ethical convictions something of value for all of civilizations. Its apprehension of God and its peculiar method of receiving and spelling out revelation in the commonplaces of everyday life were divorced from a single place, even the holiest place in the world, where they had begun.

But al-Tafāhum is wrong in supposing that the Jews "disenlandisement" was the precondition for recognition of what was of universal importance about themselves. On the contrary, it was in the Land itself that the awareness of ethnic differentiation proved the least vivid. Outside of it the group turned inward, and rightly so, for it became most acutely sensitive to its differences from others. In this respect the gentile students of Judaism do not understand what it is to be a Jew. The Diaspora Jew addresses the nations and in their own language, but in doing so speaks as a *Jew*. It is the "enlandised" Jew who sees himself or herself as no different from everyone within range of vision, therefore as human among humans, rather than Jew among gentiles. The willingness and necessity to enter into intimate relationship with each and every civilization therefore produced two sorts of encounters, the one, between the Jew in his land and others who might come there, or who might be known elsewhere, who held in common the knowledge of what it means to belong to some one place; the other, between the world and the always self-aware Jew living in other lands, a Jew sensitive to the language and experience of those lands precisely because he or she was forever at the margins of the common life.

Jewry did not disapprove the universalizing of its mission in the Church. It simply did not recognize that the Church ever truly carried out that mission. Jewry perceived no discontinuity requiring reconciliation between its sense of peoplehood (privilege) and its "self-transcending obligation." The Jews long ago ceased to be a mere ethnic continuity, and no one, in either the State of Israel or the Diaspora, regards the Jews as merely an ethnic group. One can, after all, become a Jew by other than ethnic and territorial assimilation, through *conversion*. That fact predominates in all discussions of what it is to be a Jew. The issue comes from the other side: *Can* one become a Jew not through conversion, but through mere assimilation? The dogged resistance of Jewry to the reduction of Jewishness to mere ethnicity testifies to the falseness of al-Tafāhum's reading of the Jewish situation.

But his other question is indeed troubling: Is destiny to be equated with heredity and fidelity with birth? The answer to that question can be found only in the working out of the potentialities of both Israeli and Diaspora Jewish life.

To be sure, the old Diaspora—the one before 1948—absorbed the values of the nations and could locate no one center where the distinctiveness, hence the universality, of Jewish history and civilization might be explored. Zionism does indeed posit in new and more incisive form the old question of universality, *but it also answers that question.* In the Jewish state Jews lose their sense of peculiarity. They reenter the human situation common to everyone but Jews. In the State of Israel everyone is Jewish, therefore no one is the Jew. And this, in my view, opens the way to an interesting development: the reconsideration of Jewish humanity in relationship with the other sorts of humanity in the world. It is now possible for the normal to communicate with the normal.

What the Israelis have to communicate is clear to one and all. They have not divorced themselves from important elements of the Jewish past, but have retained and enhanced them. The possession of the land, after all, represents such an important element. What does it mean to believe that one's moral life is somehow related to the destiny of the land in which one lives? In times past the question would have seemed nonsensical. But today no people is able to take its land, its environment, for granted. Everyone is required to pay attention to what one does with one's blessings. Today each land is endangered by immoral men who live upon and make use of it. The moral pollution of which the prophets spoke may infect not only a society but the way a society makes use of its resources. So the intimate relationship between Israel and the Land is no longer so alien to the existence of other nations. And the ecological-moral answers found in the Land and State of Israel are bound to have universal meaning.

I choose this example because it is the least obvious. The record of the State of Israel is, in my view, not ambiguous about "the final questions of the universal meaning and obligation of the chosen people." One need not be an Israeli apologist to recognize the numerous ways in which the State of Israel has sought to make war without fanaticism, to wage peace with selflessness.

Only indifference to the actual day to day record of the State of Israel, with its technical assistance, its thirst for peace, its fundamentally decent society at home, and above all its hatred of what it must do to survive, justifies questions concerning Israel's "universal duty." On the contrary, it seems to me that Israeli society has, within the limits of its wisdom and power, committed itself to the benediction of all peoples, and with its loyalty to that very blessing its very particularity is verified and justified.

I therefore do not agree that the new "enlandisement" has betrayed the old. It has fulfilled it.

The other half of the question pertains to the Diaspora. The Diaspora was neither the true symbol nor the tragic negation of Israel's vocation. "Chosen-ness and law, obligation to God and duty to man," are still proper and feasible clues to Jewish existence *both* at home and abroad. The Land never was, and is not now, merely the territorial locus of a secular nationality. The existence of the Diaspora guarantees otherwise. The Diaspora supplies the certainty that people of many languages and civilizations will look to Zion for more than a parochial message, just as the Israelis make certain the Diaspora Jews will hear that message. But, as I said, things are the reverse of what al-Tafāhum supposes. The Diaspora brings its acute consciousness of being different from others, therefore turns to the State to discover the ways in which it is like the others. The Diaspora contributes its variety and range of human experience to the consciousness of the State of Israel. But the State offers the Diaspora the datum of normality.

One cannot divide the Jewish people into two parts, the "enlandised" and the "disenlandised." Those in the Land look outward. Those outside look toward the Land. Those in the Land identify with the normal peoples. Those abroad see in the Land what it means to be extraordinary. But it is what happens to the whole, altogether, that is decisive for the Judaic tradition. And together, the Diaspora Jew and the Israeli represent a single tradition, a single memory. That memory is of having had a land and lost it—*and* never having repudiated either the memory of the Land *or* the experience of living elsewhere. No one in the State of Israel can imagine that to be in the Land is for the Jew what being in England is to the Englishman. The Englishman has never lost England and come back. So one cannot distinguish between the

Israeli and the Diaspora Jew. Neither one remembers or looks upon a world in which his particular values and ideals are verified by society. Neither ceases to be cosmopolitan. Both preserve a universal concern for *all* Israel. Both know diversities of culture and recognize therefore the relativity of values, even as they affirm their own.

This forms what is unique in the Jewish experience: the denial of men's need to. judge all values by their particular, self-authenticating system of thought. In this regard the Diaspora re-enforces the Israeli's view of the world, and the Israeli reciprocates. Both see as transitory and merely useful what others understand to be absolute and perfected. Behind the superficial eschatological self-confidence of Zionism lies an awareness everywhere present that that is just what Zionism adds up to: a *merely* secular eschatology. No one imagines that Zionism has completed its task or that the world has been perfected. The world is seen by both parts of the Jewish people to be insufficient and incomplete.

The Israeli's very sense of necessity preserves the Jews' neatest insight: without choice, necessity imposes duty, responsibility, unimagined possibilities. The Jews are not so foolish as to have forgotten the ancient eternal cities—theirs and others'—which are no more. They know therefore that it is not the place, but the quality of life within it, that truly matters. No city is holy, not even Jerusalem, but men and women must live in some one place and assume the responsibilities of the mundane city. But if no city is holy, at least Jerusalem may be made into a paradigm of sanctity. Though all they have for mortar may be slime, Jewish men and women will indeed build what they must, endure as they have to. The opposite is not to wander, but to die.

But have Diaspora Jews strayed so far from those same truths? In sharing the lives of many civilizations, do they do other than to assume responsibility for place? Do they see the particular city as holy, because they want to sanctify life in it? Or do they, too, know that the quality of life *anywhere* is what must truly matter? People must live in some one place and in so far as Jewish people have something to teach of all they have learned in thirty centuries, they should live and learn and teach in whatever place they love. And one may err if one underestimates the capacity of the outsider, of the Diaspora Jew, to love.

I therefore see no need either to repudiate Zionism or to give up the other elements that have made *being Jewish* a magnificent mode of humanity. Zionism, on the contrary, supplies Jewry with still another set of experiences, another set of insights into what it means to be human. Only those who repudiate the unity of Israel, the Jewish people, in favor of either of its segments can see things otherwise. But viscerally American Jews know better, and I think they are right in refusing to resolve the tensions of their several commitments. Zionism creates problems for Judaism only when Zionists think that all that being Jewish means is "enlandisement" and, thereby, redemption. But Zionists *cannot* think so when they contemplate the range of human needs and experiences they as human beings must face. Zionism is a part of Judaism. It cannot be made the whole, because Jews are more than people who need either a place to live or a place on which to focus fantasies. The profound existential necessities of Jews— both those they share with everyone and those they have to themselves—are not met by Zionism or "enlandisement" alone. Zionism provides much of the vigor and excitement of contemporary Jewish affairs, but in so far as Jews live and suffer, are born and die, reflect and doubt, raise children and worry over them, love and work—in so far as Jews are human, they require Judaism.

15

Zionism and "The Jewish Problem"

When Herzl proposed Zionism as the solution to the Jewish problem, the "Zionism" of which he spoke and the "Jewish problem" which he proposed to solve constituted chiefly political realities. But, as Arthur Hertzberg trenchantly argues in *The Zionist Idea*, Zionism actually represented not a merely secular and political ideology, but the transvaluation of Jewish values. If so, the same must be said of the "Jewish problem" to which it addresses itself. Zionism as an external force faced the world, but what shall we say of its inner spirit? The inwardness of Zionism—its "piety" and spirituality—is not to be comprehended by the world, only by the Jew, for, like the Judaism it transformed and transcended, to the world it was worldly and political, stiff-necked and stubborn (in Christian theological terms), but to the Jew it was something other, not to be comprehended by the gentile.

In his celebrated correspondence with Eugen Rosenstock-Huessy, Franz Rosenzweig wrote (in *Judaism Despite Christianity, The "Letters on Christianity and Judaism" Between Eugen Rosenstock-Huessy and Franz Rosenzweig*, ed. Eugen Rosenzweig-Huessy [University of Alabama Press, 1969]):

> ...I find that everything that I want to write is something I can't express to you. For now I would have to show you Judaism from within, that is, to be able to show it to you in a

hymn, just as you are able to show me, the outsider, Christianity. And for the very reason that you can do it, I cannot. Christianity has its soul in its externals; Judaism, on the outside, has only its hard protecting shell, and one can speak of its soul only from within . . .

Following Hertzberg, one can hardly see Zionism exept as a New Judaism, a completely new view of all that had gone before and an utterly different conception of what should come hereafter. But this Zionism—neither spiritual nor political, but in a measure a unique amalgam of the spirit and the *polis*—is hidden by its hard protecting shell. What then can we say of its soul from within?

The Zionism of which I speak is the effort to realize through political means the hope supposed to have been lost in the time of Ezekiel, proclaimed imperishable in the time of Imber, the continuous hope of restoration and renaissance first of the Land of Israel, then of the people of Israel through the Land, finally, since 1948, of the people and the Land together, wherever the people should be found. This Zionism did not come about at Basel, for its roots go back to the point in the ages at which Jewry first recognized, then rejected, its separation from the Land. Zionism is the old-new Judaism, a Judaism transformed through old-new values. It is a set of paradoxes through which the secular and the religious, separated in the nineteenth century, were again fused—re-fused—in the twentieth. Zionism to be sure is a complex phenomenon; within it are tendencies which are apt to cancel each other. But all forms of Zionism are subsumed under the definition offered here, which represents, I think, the lowest common denominator for all Zionist phenomena.

The Jewish problems which Zionism successfully solved were the consequence of the disintegration of what had been whole, the identity, consciousness, and the culture of the Jew. It was, as I said, Zionism which reconstructed the whole and reshaped the tradition in a wholly new heuristic framework.

In former times it was conventional to speak of the "Jewish problem." Most people understood that problem in political and economic terms. What shall we do about the vast Jewish populations of Eastern and Central Europe, which live a marginal economic life and have no place in the political structures of the several nations? Herzl proposed the Zionist solution to the

"Jewish problem." Dubnow wished to solve the "Jewish problem" by the creation of Jewish autonomous units in Europe. The Socialists and Communists proposed to solve the "Jewish problem" by the integration of Jewry into the movement of the international proletariat and to complete the solution of the problems of the smaller group within those of the working classes.

Today we hear less talk about the "Jewish problem" because Hitler brought it to a final solution: by exterminating the masses of European Jews, he left unsolved no social, economic, or political problems. The Western Jewries are more or less well integrated into the democratic societies. The State of Israel has no "Jewish problem" in the classic sense. The oppressed communities remaining in the Arab countries are relatively small, and the solution of their problems is to be found in migration to the West and to the State of Israel. The "Jewish problem" to be sure continues to confront Soviet Russia, and there the classic Marxist formulation of the problem still persuades people. But, for the rest, the "Jewish problem" does not describe reality or evoke a recognized, real-life perplexity. (That does not mean Jews do not have problems, or that gentiles do not have problems in relating to and understanding both Jews and Judaism.)

I shall concentrate on three aspects of the contemporary Jewish situation, all closely related, and all the result of secularism. The first is the crisis of identity, the second, the liberal dilemma, the third, the problem of self-hatred. The Jewish identity crisis may be simply stated: There is no consensus shared by most Jews about what a Jew is, how Judaism should be defined, what "being Jewish" and "Judaism" are supposed to mean for individuals and the community. The liberal dilemma is this: How can I espouse universal principles and yet remain part of a particular community? The problem of self-hatred needs little definition, but provokes much illustration, for many of the phenomena of contemporary Jewish life reflect the low self-esteem attached to being Jewish.

For Jews the secular revolution is not new. From the Haskalah, the Jewish Enlightenment in the eighteenth century, onward, Jews have come forward to propose a nonreligious interpretation of "being Jewish," an interpretation divorced from the classic mythic structure of Judaism. The God-Is-Dead movement evoked little response among Jewish theologians and ideologists because they found nothing new in it. If the issue was naturalistic, instead of supernatural, theology, Jewish theologians had heard Mordecai Kaplan for half-a-century or more. If the issue was atheism, it had been formulated by Jewish secularists, socialists, and assimilationists in various ways from the mid–nineteenth century forward. If the secular revolution means that large numbers of people cease to look to religion, or to religious institutions, for the meaning of their lives and cease to practice religious traditions and to affirm religious beliefs, then this is neither news nor a revolution. Jews have participated in that sort of "revolution" for two centuries. They have done so without ceasing to regard themselves, and to be regarded by others, as Jews. That does not mean the Jews have found antidotes to the secular fever, but it does mean that they by now have a considerable heritage of experience, a substantial corpus of cases and precedents, for what Christians find to be new and revolutionary: the loosing of the world from all religious and supernatural interpretations.

The secular revolution has imposed upon Jews a profound crisis of identity. In former times everyone knew who was a Jew and what being a Jew meant. A Jew was a member of a religious nation, living among other nations by its own laws, believing in Torah revealed at Sinai and in one God who had chosen Israel, and hoping for the coming of the Messiah. The gentile world shared the philosophical presuppositions of Jewish beliefs. Everyone believed in God. Everyone believed in prophecy, in revelation, in the Jews' holy book. Everyone believed in the coming of the Messiah. Above all, everyone interpreted reality by supernaturalist principles. To be sure groups differed on the nature of God, the particular prophets to be regarded as true, the book God had revealed. But these differences took place within a vast range of agreement.

When religious understandings of the world lost their hold on masses of Western people, "being Jewish" became as problematical as any other aspect of archaic reality. If to be Jewish meant to be part of a Jewish religious community, then when Jews ceased to believe in religious propositions, they ought to have ceased being Jewish. Yet that is not what happened. For several generations Jewish atheists and agnostics have continued to take an active role in the Jewish community—indeed, functionally to constitute the majority in it—and have seen nothing unusual either in their participation in Jewish life or in their lack of religious commitment. Indeed today the American Jewish community is nearly unique in interpreting "being Jewish" primarily in religious, or at least rhetorically religious, terms. Other Jewish communities see themselves as a community, a nation, a people, whether or not religion plays a role in defining what is particular about that community. The secular revolution immensely complicated the definition of Jewish identity, not only by breaking down the uniform classical definition, but also by supplying a variety of new, complex definitions in its place.

Today, therefore, if we ask ouselves, "What are the components of 'Jewishness'?" we are hard put to find an answer. What are the attitudes, associations, rituals both secular and religious, psychology and culture, which both Jews and others conceive to be Jewish? The truth is, today there is no such thing as a single Jewish identity, as there assuredly was in times past an identity one could define in meaningful terms. Jewishness now is a function of various social and cultural settings, and is meaningful in those settings only.

The Jews obviously are not a nation in the accepted sense; but they also are hardly a people in the sense that an outsider can investigate or understand the components of that peoplehood. There is no "Jewish way" of organizing experience and interpreting reality, although there was and is a Judaic way. There is no single Jewish ideology, indeed no single, unitary Jewish history, although there once was a cogent Judaic theology and a Judaic view of a unitary and meaningful progression of events to be called "Jewish history." Only if we impose upon discrete events of scarcely related groups in widely separated places and ages the concept of a single unitary history can we speak of "Jewish history." Jewish peoplehood in a concrete, secular, this-worldly historical sense is largely a matter of faith, that is, the construction of historians acting as do theologians in other settings. There once was a single Jewish ideological system, a coherent body of shared images, ideas and ideals, which provided for participants a coherent overall orientation in space and time, in means and ends. There once was such a system, but in the secular revolution it has collapsed.

It is indeed, the secular revolution that has imposed on Jewry a lingering crisis of identity. Jews today may find in common a set of emotions and responses. These do not constitute an "identity," but rather, a set of common characteristics based upon differing verbal explanations and experiences. That does not mean no one knows what a Jew is. In particular settings Jews *can* be defined and understood in terms applicable to those settings. But as an abstraction the "Jewish people" is a theological or ideological construct not to be imposed upon the disparate, discrete data known as Jews or even as Jewish communities in various times and places. Lacking a common language and culture, even a common religion, the Jews do not have what they once had. Today Jewish identity so greatly varies that we need to reconsider the viability of the very concept of "Jewishness" as a universal attribute, for today Jewishness cannot be defined in neutral, cultural terms.

If there are no inherent and essential Jewish qualities in the world, then nothing about "being Jewish" is natural, to be taken for granted. Being Jewish becomes something one must achieve, define, strive for. It is today liberated from the forms and content of the recent past, from the "culture-Judaism" of the American and Canadian Jewish communities. If the artifacts of that "culture-Judaism"—matters of cuisine, or philanthropy, or cliquishness—are not part of some immutable and universal Jewish identity, then they may well be criticized from within, not merely abandoned and left behind in disgust. One can freely repudiate them in favor of other ways.

Omissions in contemporary Jewish "identity" are as striking as the inclusions. Among the things taken for granted are a sense of group loyalty, a desire to transmit "pride in Judaism" to the next generation, in sum a desire to survive. But the identity of large numbers of Jews, whether they regard themselves as secular or not, does not include a concept of God, of the meaning of life, of the direction and purpose of history. The uncriticized, but widely accepted Jewish identity syndrome is formed of the remnants of the piety of the recent past, a piety one may best call residual, cultural, and habitual, rather than self-conscious, critical, and theological (or ideological). That identity is not even ethnic, but rather a conglomeration of traits picked up in particular historical and social experiences. It is certainly flat and one-dimensional, leaving Jews to wander in strange paths in search of the answers to the most fundamental human perplexities.

Why are Jews in the forefront of universal causes, to the exclusion of their own interest and identity? Charles Liebman, writing in *The Religious Situation 1969,* examines the reasons given for this phenomenon. He rejects the notion that Jewish liberalism, cosmopolitanism, and internationalism rest on "traditional" Jewish values, for, he points out, it is the secular, not the religious, Jew who espouses cosmopolitanism. Jewish religious values in fact are folk-oriented rather than universalistic.

Liebman likewise rejects the view that the Jews' social status, far below what they might anticipate from their economic attainments, accounts for their attraction to the fringes of politics. This theory accounts, Liebman says, for Jewish radicalism rather than Jewish liberalism, that is, for only a small element of the community. Further, Jewish radicals normally abandon Jewish community life; the liberals dominate it.

A third explanation derives from the facts of history. Liberal parties supported the emancipation of the Jews; conservative ones opposed it. But for the U.S. this was not the case. Indeed, until the New Deal, Jews tended to be Republican, not Democratic or Socialist. Liebman posits that the appeal of liberalism is among Jews estranged from the religious tradition. This appeal, he says, "lies in the search for a universalistic ethic to which a Jew can adhere *but* which is seemingly irrelevant to specific Jewish concerns and, unlike radical socialism, does not demand total commitment at the expense of all other values."

Since the Emancipation, Jews have constantly driven to free themselves from the condition which Judaism thrusts on them. This Liebman calls estrangement: "The impetus for intellectual and religious reform among Jews, the adoption of new ideologies and life styles, but above all else the changing self-perception by the Jew of himself and his condition was not simply a desire to find amelioration from the physical oppression of the ghetto. It was rather a desire for emancipation from the very essence of the Jewish condition. . . . The Jew's problem was his alienation from the roots and the traditions of the society."

Here is the point at which the phenomenon of secularization becomes important. Jews earlier knew they were different, estranged. But with the collapse of religious evaluations of difference, the Jews ceased to affirm that difference. Secularization changed the nature of the Jew's perception of his condition, transferred the estrangement from theology to the realm of contemporary culture and civilization.

Jews supported universal humanism and cosmopolitanism with a vengeance. They brought these ideals home to the community so that Jewish difference was played down. Look, for example, at the Union Prayerbook, and count the number of times the congregation prays for "all mankind." The New Liberal Prayerbook in England so emphasizes the universal to the exclusion of the particular that one might write to the English liberal rabbi responsible for the liturgy: "Warm and affectionate regards to your wife and children, and to all mankind." Liebman concludes, "The Jew wished to be accepted as an equal in society *not* because he was a Jew, but because his Jewishness was *irrelevant*. Yet at the same time, the Jew refused to make his own Jewishness irrelevant. . . . He made . . . contradictory demands on society. He wants to be accepted into the tradition of society without adapting to the society's dominant tradition." This constitutes the liberal dilemma: how to affirm universalism and remain particular.

However complex the liberal identity of secular Jews, it is still more complicated by the phenomena of anti-Semitism and consequent self-hatred. The "Jewish problem" is most commonly phrased by young Jews as, Why should I be Jewish? I believe in universal ideals—who needs particular ones as well?

Minorities feel themselves "particular," see their traditions as "ritual," and distinguish between the private, unique, and personal and the public, universal and commonplace. Majorities do not. Standing at the center, not on the fringe, they accept the given. Those who are marginal, as the Jews are, regard the given as something to be criticized, elevated, in any event distinguished from their own essential being.

Jews who ask, Why be Jewish? testify that "being Jewish" somehow repels, separates persons from the things they want. American society, though it is opening, still is not so open that those who are different from the majority can serenely and happily accept that difference. True, they frequently affirm it—but the affirmation contains such excessive protest that it is not much different from denial. The quintessential datum of American Jewish existence is anti-Semitism, along with uncertainty of status, denial of normality, and self-doubt. The results are many, but two stand out. Some overemphasize their Jewishness, respond to it not naturally but excessively, to the exclusion of other parts of their being. Others question and implicitly deny it. The one compensates too much; the other finds no reward at all.

As Kurt Lewin pointed out in *Resolving Social Conflicts: Selected Papers on Group Dynamics* [N.Y.: Harper, 1948]), ".... every underprivileged minority group is kept together not only by cohesive forces among its members but also by the boundary which the majority erects against the crossing of an individual from the minority to the majority group." An underprivileged group member will try to gain in social status by joining the majority—to pass, to assimilate. The basic fact of life is this wish to cross the boundary, and hence, as Lewin says, "he [the minority group member] lives almost perpetually in a state of conflict and tension. He dislikes... his own group because it is nothing but a burden to him. ... A Jew of this type will dislike everything specifically Jewish, for he will see in it that which keeps him away from the majority for which he is longing." Such a Jew is the one who will constantly ask, Why be Jewish?—who will see, or at least fantasize about, a common religion of humanity, universalism or universal values that transcend, and incidentally obliterate, denominational and sectarian boundaries. It is no accident that the universal language, Esperanto, the universal movement, Communism, the universal psychology, Freudianism, all were in large measure attractive to marginal Jews.

True, Jews may find a place in social groups indifferent to their particularity as Jews. But a closer look shows that these groups are formed chiefly by deracinated, dejudaized Jews, along with a few exceptionally liberal non-Jews standing in a similar relationship to their own origins. Jews do assimilate. They do try to blot out the marks of their particularity, in ways more sophisticated, to be sure, than the ancient Hellenistic Jews who submitted to painful operations to wipe away the marks of circumcision. But in doing so, they become not something else entirely, but another type of Jew. The real issue is never, to be or not to be a Jew, any more than it is, to be or not to be my father's son.

Lewin makes this wholly clear: "It is not similarity or dissimilarity of individuals that constitutes a group, but interdependence of fate." Jews brought up to suppose being Jewish is chiefly, or only, a matter of religion think that through atheism they cease to be Jews, only to discover that disbelieving in God helps not at all. They still are Jews. They still are obsessed by that fact and compelled to confront it, whether under the name of Warren or of Weinstein, whether within the society of Jews or elsewhere.

Indeed, outside of that society Jewish consciousness becomes most intense. Among Jews one is a human being, with peculiarities and virtues of one's own. Among gentiles he is a Jew, with traits common to the group he rejects. That is probably why Jews still live in mostly Jewish neighborhoods and associate, outside of economic life, mostly with other Jews, whether or not these associations exhibit traits supposed to be Jewish. And when crisis comes, as it frequently does, then no one doubts that he or she shares a common cause, a common fate, with other Jews. Then it is hardest to isolate oneself from Jews, because only among Jewry are these intense concerns shared.

The Jewish community has yet to face up to the self-hatred endemic in its life. Jews are subtle enough to explain they are too busy with non-Jewish activities to associate with Jews. Students coming to college do not say to themselves or others, "I do not want to be a Jew, and now that I have the chance not to be, I shall take it." They say, "I do not like the Hillel rabbi; I am not religious so won't go to services; I am too busy with studies, dates, or political and social programs to participate in Jewish life." From here it is a short step to the affirmation of transcendent, universal values, and the denial of particular "religious" identity. That those who take that step do so mostly with other Jews is, as I said, proof of the real intent.

The organized Jewish community differs not at all from the assimilationist sector of this student generation. Indeed, it shows the way. Leadership in Jewry is sought by talented and able people, particularly those whose talents and abilities do not produce commensurate results in the non-Jewish world. Status denied elsewhere is readily available, for the right reasons, in Jewry, but in Jewry status is measured by the values of the gentile establishment.

Lewin says, "In any group, those sections are apt to gain

leadership which are more generally successful. In a minority group, individual members who are economically success-ful...usually gain a higher degree of acceptance by the majority group. This places them culturally on the periphery of the under-privileged group and makes them more likely to be 'marginal' persons.... Nevertheless, they are frequently called for leader-ship by the underprivileged group because of their status and power. They themselves are usually eager to accept the leading role in the minority, partly as a substitute for gaining status in the majority. As a result, we find the rather paradoxical phenomenon of what one might call 'the leader from the periphery.' Instead of having a group led by people who are proud of the group, who wish to stay in it and to promote it, we see minority leaders who are lukewarm toward to the group..." This, I think, is very much true of U.S. Jewry.

American Jews want to be Jewish, but not too much so, not so much that they cannot be just "people," part of the imaginary undifferentiated majority. And herein lies their pathology: they suppose one one can distinguish between one's Jewishness, hu-manity, personality, individuality, and religion. Human beings, however, do not begin as part of an undifferentiated mass. Once they leave the maternity ward, they go to a home of real people with a history, a home that comes from somewhere and that was made by some specific people. They inherit the psychic, not to mention social and cultural, legacy of many generations.

What has Zionism to do with these Jewish problems? It is, after all, supposedly a secular movement, called "secular mes-sianism," and the problems I have described are the conse-quences of secularity. How then has an allegedly secular move-ment posited solutions to the challenges of secularity faced by the formerly religious community?

Zionism provides a reconstruction of Jewish identity, for it reaffirms the nationhood of Israel in the face of the disintegration of the religious bases of Jewish peoplehood. If in times past the Jews saw themselves as a people because they were the children of the promise, the children of Abraham, Isaac, and Jacob, called together at Sinai, instructed by God through prophets, led by rabbis guided by the "whole Torah"—written and oral—of Sinai, then with the end of a singularly religious self-consciousness, the people lost its understanding of itself. The fact is that the people remained a community of fate, but, until the flourishing of Zionism, the facts of its continued existence were deprived of a heuristic foundation. Jews continued as a group, but could not persuasively say why or what this meant. Zionism provided the explanation: The Jews indeed remain a people, but the foundation of their peoplehood lies in the unity of their concern for Zion, in devotion to rebuilding the Land and establishing Jewish sovereignty in it. The realities of continuing emotional and social commitment to Jewish "grouphood" or separateness thus made sense. Mere secular difference, once seen to be destiny—"who has not made us like the nations"—once again stood forth as destiny.

Herein lies the ambiguity of Zionism. It was supposedly a secular movement, yet in reinterpreting the classic mythic structures of Judaism, it compromised its secularity and exposed its fundamental unity with the classic mythic being of Judaism. If, as I suggested, groups with like attributes do not necessarily represent "peoples" or "nations," and if the common attributes, in the Jewish case, are neither intrinsically Jewish (whatever that might mean) nor widely present to begin with, then the primary conviction of Zionism constitutes an extraordinary reaffirmation of the primary element in the classical mythic structure: salvation. What has happened in Zionism is that the old has been in one instant destroyed and resurrected. The holy people are no more, the nation-people take their place. How much has changed in the religious tradition, when the allegedly secular successor continuator has preserved not only the essential perspective of the tradition, but done so pretty much in the tradition's own symbols and language?

Nor should it be supposed that the Zionist solution to the Jews' crisis of identity is a merely theological or ideological one. We cannot ignore the practical result of Zionist success in conquering the Jewish community. For the middle and older generations, as everyone knows, the Zionist enterprise provided the primary vehicle for Jewish identity. The Reform solution to the identity problem—we are Americans by nationality, Jews by religion—was hardly congruent to the profound Jewish passion of the immigrant generations and their children. The former generations were *not* merely Jewish by religion. Religion was the least important aspect of their Jewishness. They deeply felt themselves

Jewish in their bone and marrow and did not feel sufficiently marginal as Jews to *need* to affirm their Americanness/Judaism at all. Rather they participated in a reality; they were in a situation so real and intimate as to make unnecessary such an uncomfortable, defensive affirmation. They did not doubt they were Americans. They did not need to explain what being Jewish had to do with it. Zionism was congruent to these realities, and because of that fact, being Jewish and being Zionist were inextricably joined together.

But how different is the newer generation? True, extreme aberrant Jewish elements in the New Left are prepared to turn against the State of Israel. But what, more than anything else, has weakened the New Left and caused its split into numerous bickering factions, if not the defection of considerable numbers of Jewish radicals, unable to stomach both the crude anti-Semitism and the mindless pro-Nasserism of the Communist-line New Left groups? If so, we can only conclude that the younger generation is as viscerally Zionist as the older generations. The rock on which the New Left split was none other than 1967 Zion. I cannot think of more striking evidence of the persistence of the Zionist conception of Jewish identity among the younger generation.

The Zionist critique of the Jews' liberal dilemma is no less apt. Zionism has not stood against liberal causes and issues. On the contrary, Zionist Socialists have stood at the forefront of the liberal cause, have struggled for the working-class ideals, have identified the working class cause with their own. The record of Israeli and American Zionist thought on liberal issues is unambiguous and consistent. The liberalism of which Liebman writes is of a different order. It is a liberalism not born in Jewish nationhood but despite and against it. The liberal cosmopolitan Jew, devoted to internationalist and universal causes to the exclusion of "parochial" Jewish concerns, is no Zionist, but the opposite. He or she is a Jew acting out the consequences of deracination in the political arena. His or her universal liberalism takes the place of a profound commitment to the Jews and their welfare. Indeed, it is a liberalism that would like to deny that Jews have special, particular interests and needs to begin with. "Struggling humanity" in all its forms but one claims his sympathy: when Jews suffer, they *have* to do so as part of undifferentiated humanity.

In so far as this Jewish liberalism was nonsectarian and hostile to the things that concern Jews as Jews—as in those Jewish welfare federations which articulately state their purpose as humanitarian to the exclusion of Judaism—Zionism has rejected that liberalism. It has done so because of its critical view of the Emancipation. Unlike the Jewish liberals, Zionism saw the Emancipation as a problem, not a solution. It was dubious of its promises and aware of its hypocrisies. It saw Emancipation as a threat to Jewry and in slight measure a benefit for Jews. The Jews' problem was that Emancipation represented dejudaization. The price of admission to the roots and traditions of "society" was the surrender of the roots and traditions of the Jew, so said Zionist thought.

At the same time Zionism stood between the religious party, which utterly rejected Emancipation and its works, and the secular-reform-liberal party, which wholly affirmed them. It faced the reality of Emancipation without claiming in its behalf a messianic valence. Emancipation is here, therefore to be criticized, but coped with; not utterly rejected, like the Orthodox, nor wholeheartedly affirmed, like the secular, reform, and liberal groups. Zionism therefore demanded that the Jew be accepted as an equal in society because he or she was a Jew, *not* because Jewishness was irrelevant. Its suspicion of the liberal stance was based, correctly, in my opinion, on the Jews' ambivalence toward Jewishness. Zionism clearly recognized that the Jewishness of the Jew could never be irrelevant, not to the gentile, not to the Jew. It therefore saw more clearly than the liberals the failures of the European Emancipation and the dangers of American liberalism to Jewish self-respect and Jewish interests. Zionists were quick to perceive the readiness of non-Jewish allies of Jewish liberals to take the Jewish liberals at their word: We Jews have no special interests, nothing to fight for in our own behalf. Zionists saw Jews had considerable interests, just like other groups, and exposed the self-deceit (or hypocrisy) of those who said otherwise. The liberal Jew wanted to be accepted into the traditions of society without complete assimilation, on the one side, but also without much Jewishness, on the other. The Zionist assessment of the situation differed, as I said, for it saw that Jews could achieve a place in the common life *only* as Jews; and, rightly for Europe, it held this was impossible.

In its gloomy assessment of the European Emancipation,

Zionism found itself in a position to cope with the third component in the Jewish problem, the immense, deep-rooted, and wide-ranging self-hatred of Jews. The Zionist affirmation of Jewish peoplehood, of Jewish being, stood in stark contrast to the inability of marginal and liberal Jews to cope with anti-Semitism. Cases too numerous to list demonstrate the therapeutic impact of Zionism on the faltering psychological health of European Jews, particularly of more sensitive and intellectual individuals.

The American situation is different in degree, for here anti-Semitism in recent times has made its impact in more subtle ways, but its presence is best attested by the Jews themselves. Yet if a single factor in the self-respect American Jewry does possess can be isolated, it is its pride in the State of Israel and its achievements. Zionism lies at the foundation of American Jewry's capacity to affirm its Jewishness. Without Zionism religious conviction, forced to bear the whole burden by itself, would prove a slender reed. To be a Jew "by religion," and to make much of that fact in an increasingly secular environment, would not represent an attractive option to many. The contributions to Jewry's psychological health by the State of Israel and the Zionist presence in the Diaspora cannot be overestimated. It is striking, for example, that Kurt Lewin, Milton Steinberg, and other students of the phenomena of Jewish self-hatred invariably reached the single conclusion that only through Zionism would self-hatred by mitigated, even overcome.

The role of Zionism as a therapy for self-hatred cannot be described only in terms of the public opinion of U.S. Jewry. That would tell us much about the impact of mass communications, but little about the specific value of the Zionist idea for healing the Jewish pathology. In my view, the Israelis' claim "to live a full Jewish life" is a valid one. In Zionist conception and Israeli reality, the Jew is indeed a thoroughly integrated, whole human being. Here, in conception and reality, the Jew who believes in justice, truth, and peace, in universal brotherhood and dignity, does so not despite his or her peculiarity as a Jew, but through it, making no distinction between Jewishness, humanity, individuality, way of living, and ultimate values. These constitute a single, undivided and fully integrated existential reality.

Part of the reason is the condition of life: The State of Israel is the largest Jewish neighborhood in the world. But part of the reason is ideological, and not merely circumstantial: Zionists always have rejected the possibility of Jews' "humanity" without Jewishness, just as they denied the reality of distinctions between Jewishness, nationality and faith. They were not only *not* Germans of the Mosaic persuasion, but also *not* human beings of the Jewish genus. The several sorts of bifurcations attempted by non-Zionists to account for their Jewishness along with other sorts of putatively non-Jewish commitments and loyalties were rejected by Zionists. It was not that Zionists did not comprehend the dilemmas faced by other sorts of Jews, but rather that they supposed through Zionism they had found the solution. They correctly held that through Zionist ideology and activity they had overcome the disintegrating Jewish identity crisis of others.

At the outset I suggested that, like Judaism, Zionism can be understood from within, from its soul. My claim is that Zionism is to be understood as a solution to Jewish problems best perceived by the Jews who face those problems. The "Jewish problem" imposed by the effects of secularism took the form of a severe and complex crisis of identity, a partial commitment to universalism and cosmopolitan liberalism while claiming the right to be a little different, and a severe psychopathological epidemic of self-hatred. But the way Zionism actually solved those problems is more difficult to explain. If, as I suppose, because of Zionism contemporary Jewries have a clearer perception of who they are, what their interests consist of, and of their value as human beings, then Zionism and the State of Israel are in substantial measure the source of the saving knowledge. But *how* has Zionism worked its salvation on the Jews? Here I think we come to realities only Jews can understand. They understand them *not* because of rational reflection but because of experience and unreflective, natural response.

Zionism, and Zionism alone, proved capable of interpreting to contemporary Jews the meaning of felt history, *and* of doing so in terms congruent to what the Jews derived from their tradition. It was Zionism which properly assessed the limitations of the Emancipation and proposed sound and practical programs to cope with those limitations. It was Zionism which gave Jews strength to affirm themselves when faced with the anti-Semitism of European and American life in the first half of the twentieth century. It was Zionism and that alone which showed a way forward from the nihilism and despair of the D.P. camps. It was Zionism and that alone which provided a basis for unity in U.S. Jewry in the fifties and sixties of this century, a ground for common action among otherwise utterly divided groups.

These achievements of Zionism were based not on their practicality, though Zionism time and again was proved "right" by history. The Jews were moved and responded to Zionism before, not after the fact. And they were moved because of the capacity of Zionism to resurrect the single most powerful force in the history of Judaism: Messianism. Zionism did so in ways too numerous to list, but the central fact is that it represented, as Hertzberg perceptively showed, not "secular Messianism" but a profound restatement in new ways of classical Messianism. Zionism recovered the old, still evocative messianic symbolism and imagery and filled them with new meaning. And *this* meaning was taken for granted by vast numbers of Jews because it accurately described not what they believed or hoped for—not faith—but rather what they took to be mundane reality. Zionism took within its heuristic framework each and every important event in twentieth-century Jewish history and gave to all a single, comprehensive, and sensible interpretation. Events were no longer random or unrelated, but all were part of a single pattern, pointing toward an attainable messianic result. It was not the random degradation of individuals in Germany and Poland, not the meaningless murder of unfortunates, not the creation of another state in the Middle East. All of these events were related to one another. It was Holocaust and rebirth, and the state was the State of *Israel*.

In so stating the meaning of contemporary events, Zionism made it possible for Jews not only to understand what they witnessed, but to draw meaning from it. And even more, Zionism breathed new life into ancient Scriptures, by providing a contemporary interpretation—subtle and not fundamentalist to be sure—for the prophets. "Our hope is lost," Ezekiel denied in the name of God. "Our hope is not lost," was the response of Zionism. These things were no accident, still less the result of an exceptionally clever publicist's imagination. They demonstrate the center and core of Zionist spirituality and piety: the old-new myth of peoplehood, land, redemption above all. The astonishing achievements of Zionism are the result of the capacity of Zionism to reintegrate the tradition with contemporary reality, to do so in an entirely factual, matter-of-fact framework, thus to eschew faith and to elicit credence. Zionism speaks in terms of Judaic myth, indeed so profoundly that myth and reality coincide.

Glossary

Ahad Ha'Am	Zionist philosopher (1856–1927), "One of the People," whose name was Asher Hirsch Ginsberg. He espoused the position that the purpose of creating Jewish settlements in what was then Palestine was to form a spiritual center" for the Jewish people throughout the world.
Alenu	"It is incumbent upon us," the opening words of the prayer with which formal Jewish worship concludes morning, afternoon, and evening. The stress is on God's having chosen Israel and distinguished Israel from the nations.
Aliyah	Immigration to the State of Israel. Literally: "ascent," as in the Pilgrim Psalms, which speak of ascent to Jerusalem and the Holy Temple. See *Yeridah.*
Anomic	Standing out of meaningful interrelationships with other people; the absence of significant personal ties to other people; a sense of loneliness and alienation. A category of sociology.
Cathectic	The opposite of anomic, the capacity to enter into close and intense human relationships;

	the eagerness to relate to other people. A category of psychology.
Enlandisement	Tying up a religious tradition to a particular place; treating Judaism as the religion of a particular land, first and foremost. See *locative, utopian*.
Eretz Yisrael	The Land of Israel, the Holy Land, in contradistinction to everywhere else. Jews tend to avoid referring to the Holy Land as Palestine," and prefer to speak of the Land. In Hebrew, a reference to "our Land," can mean only the Land of Israel; Americans speaking in Hebrew of America are ill-advised to use *artzenu* ("our land") in this context.
Galut	The state of being in exile, suffering from alienation.
Golah	Exile. For Jews, everywhere outside of the Land of Israel. Sometimes people refer to "the Diaspora" or "the dispersion," but in Zionist language, all Jews outside of the State of Israel are in *Golah*, that is, they are physically located in exile, and therefore also are in the situation of *Galut*, that is, spiritually located in exile.
Goyim	Gentiles: not always pejorative.
Halakhah	The Jewish way of life; law. The *halakhah*, or Jewish law, describes how things are to be done and how they are properly done.
Hasalah purta	A "diminished salvation," a small attainment.
Heilsgeschichte	The history of salvation; a religious view of events; the story of how people are saved.
Judah the Patriarch	The political authority of the Jews of the Land of Israel at the end of the second century of the Common Era (C.E. = A.D.); Judah the Patriarch is responsible for the promulgation of the Mishnah.
Kabbalistic	Pertaining to the Kabbalah, the tradition of mystical speculation and practice in Judaism.

Glossary

Locative Stressing location; emphasizing a particular place, e.g., land, in which what happens is important because it happens in that particular place. The antonym is utopian, that is, no-place, stressing what happens and is relevant everywhere. The use of utopian and locative in this sense is, to my knowledge, first found in the writings of Professor Jonathan Z. Smith, The University of Chicago. Compare "en-landisement."

Masada The place in which the Jewish army led by Bar Kokhba made its last stand against the Romans in the Second War against Rome, 132–*135*.

Mishnah The law code promulgated by Judah the Patriarch, which forms the foundation and constitution of Judaism as the basis for the two Talmuds (Babylonian, Palestinian). The Mishnah came to closure about 200 and generated the work which culminated in the Palestinian (Jerusalem) Talmud, ca. 450, and the Babylonian Talmud, ca. 500–600.

Myth A story which tells the truth about how things are and how they came to be as they are; an account of the deepest meaning in the form of a tale or a narrative about sacred or holy events. This usage is standard in the study of religions and routine here. The use of myth in the sense of "lies about the gods," and, by extension, lies in general, plays no role in this book.

Qibbutz galuyyot The in-gathering of the exiles. In Judaic prayer and theology, this in-gathering is supposed to take place at the end of time and to be accomplished in the messianic age, when all Israel will be reassembled in the Holy Land. In Zionist and Israeli terms the reference is to the immigration (*aliyah*, "ascent") of whole Jewish communities from various places.

Rav | A Talmudic rabbi who studied in the Land of Israel and immigrated to Babylonia toward the beginning of the third century; one of the founders of the Babylonian Talmud.

Samuel | A Talmudic rabbi who was raised in Babylonia, and, along with Rav, was one of the principal figures in the formative strata of the Babylonian Talmud.

Shelilat hagolah | The negation of the exilic communities, the position that the Jews outside of the State of Israel are destined to go out of existence, either through ultimate assimilation or through another "Holocaust," or both ("singing Christmas carols in the gas chambers"); the view that nothing of value or permanent worth has ever come, or can ever come, from Jews who live outside of the Land and State of Israel; the position that any effort to secure the continuing existence of the communities of the *Golah* is hopeless, worthless, and contrary to the interests of Zionism and the Jewish State. An extreme expression of Zionism.

Shomer Yisrael | In Psalms, the Guardian of Israel, namely, God. In the Israel Bond campaign, a person who purchases a $1,000 Israel Bond.

Shtetl | Yiddish word for village; particularly, a small village, inhabited mostly by Jews, on the plains of Eastern Europe.

Tanakh | The Hebrew Scriptures, formed of the acronym *Torah*, Pentateuch, *Nebi'im*, Prophets, *Ketubim*, Writings, hence TaNaKH. For Christians: "the Old Testament."

Torah | Judaism.

Tekoa | Village where Amos lived.

Glossary

Tzitzit	Show-fringes, required for the prayer shawl. Orthodox Jews wear show-fringes on a separate undergarment.
Utopia	No-where. Utopian: Pertaining to no particular place.
Yavneh	*See* Yohanan ben Zakkai.
Yeshiva	Place for ritual learning of the Talmud.
Yeridah	Emigration from the State of Israel. Literally: "descent."
Yishuv	The Jewish community of Palestine before the creation of the State of Israel in 1948. Sometimes "the old Yishuv" is used to refer to the Jewish community of Palestine before the advent of the Zionist movement.
Yohanan ben Zakkai	After the destruction of the Temple in 70, the principal figure in the surviving generation of sages. Yohanan ben Zakkai is supposed to have taken refuge in Yavneh, a coastal town in the southern part of the Land of Israel, where he assembled disciples and reestablished a center for the teaching and practice of Judaism. "Yavneh" thus symbolizes the reformation of Judaism after the catastrophe of 70 and serves as a symbol for the reconstruction of the Jewish world after a great disaster.
586 B.C.E.	The date of the destruction of the First Temple of Jerusalem by the Babylonians.
70 C.E.	The date of the destruction of the Second Temple of Jerusalem by the Romans.
1948	The date of the founding of the State of Israel by the Jews.

Index